COLOSSIANS

AND

PHILEMON

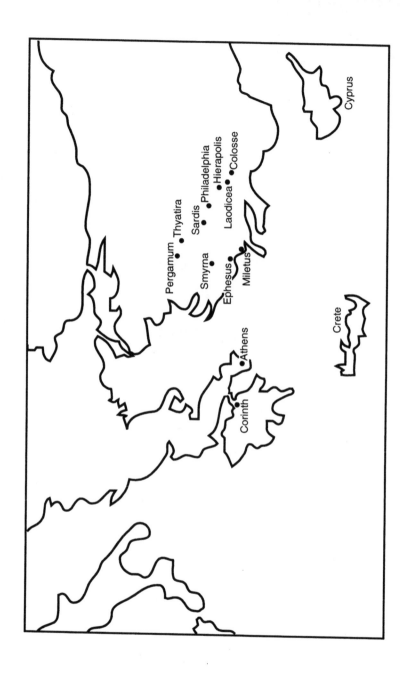

COLOSSIANS
AND
PHILEMON

Michael Bentley

EVANGELICAL PRESS

EVANGELICAL PRESS
Faverdale North Industrial Estate, Darlington, DL3 0PH,
England

Evangelical Press USA
P. O. Box 84, Auburn, MA 01501, USA

e-mail: sales@evangelical-press.org

web: http://www.evangelicalpress.org

First published 2002

British Library Cataloguing in Publication Data available

ISBN 0 85234 489 9

Printed and bound in Great Britain by Creative Print & Design
Wales, Ebbw Vale

To

Anais Tiri Bentley,
Walkworth, New Zealand
May Anais, born 10 July 2001,
grow up to know the fulness of Christ.

CONTENTS

HOW TO USE *THE GUIDE*

Colossians and Philemon is the third book in a new series called *The Guide*. The series itself covers other books of the Bible on an individual basis, such as *The Guide — Ecclesiastes*, and relevant topics such as *The Guide to Christian comfort*. The series aim is to communicate the Christian faith in a straightforward and readable way.

Each book in *The Guide* will cover a book of the Bible or topic in some detail, but will be contained in relatively short and concise chapters. There will be questions at the end of each chapter for personal study or group discussion, to help you to study the Word of God more deeply.

An innovative and exciting feature of *The Guide* is that it is linked to its own web site. As well as being encouraged to search God's Word for yourself, you are invited to ask questions related to the book on the web site, where you will not only be able to have your own questions answered, but also be able to see a selection of answers that have been given to other readers. The web site can be found at www.evangelicalpress.org/TheGuide. Once you are on the site you just need to click on the 'select' button at the top of the page, according to the book on which you wish to post a question. Your question will then be answered either by Michael Bentley, the web site co-ordinator and author of *The Guide — Colossians and Philemon*, or others who have been selected because of their experience, their understanding of the Word of God and their dedication to working for the glory of the Lord.

There are two other books being published with *The Guide — Colossians and Philemon*, they are: *The Guide — The Bible book by book* and *The Guide — Ecclesiastes*, and many more will follow. It is the publisher's hope that you will be stirred up to think more deeply about the Christian faith, and will be helped and encouraged in living out your Christian life, through the study of God's Word, in the difficult and demanding days in which we live.

CHAPTER ONE

WRITING THE LETTER TO THE CHURCH AT COLOSSE

BIBLE READING

The letter to the Colossians

Many believe that it was while Paul was confined at Rome that he wrote the letters to the churches at Ephesus, Colosse and Philippi, and also the personal one to Philemon. One day, around the years A. D. 60-62, the apostle had a visitor. The traveller had come from the Roman province of Asia Minor (called Turkey today). This, no doubt, prompted Paul to recall the two years he had spent in the city of Ephesus, which lay several hundred miles to the east of Rome. During that time, many people came to hear the apostle preach the gospel of salvation through faith in Christ Jesus (Acts 19:10). Included in that number was the man who stood before him. He had come from the church that met at the town of Colosse. Paul's constant concern was for the welfare of all the churches (2 Corinthians 11:28). So his mind would have gone to each of the Christian groups in that area, and even to Colosse which he had never personally visited.

The town of Colosse lay some miles to the east of Ephesus. It stood on the banks of the Lycus

River. It had been very important in earlier years because it lay on the great east-west trade route, leading from Ephesus on the Aegean Sea to the Euphrates River. However, by the time of Paul, its influence had diminished in favour of the growing cities of Laodicea and Hierapolis (Colossians 4:13), which lay a short distance away. Because of its central location, Ephesus was important to the whole region. It is likely that during Paul's two years of ministry in that major city, many people would have travelled from the regions around to hear him teach God's Word, and also to have personal interviews with him.

SUMMARIZE IT

We have seen so far that the apostle Paul wrote the Colossian letter when he was in prison. Although Paul had never visited this town in Asia Minor (now Turkey), he would have known a great deal about the church because he spent two full years working near Ephesus.

PRACTICAL TASKS

1. Look at the map (see page 2) and notice how many towns on it are mentioned in the New Testament.

2. Find the locations of the seven churches to which Jesus wrote letters (Revelation 2 - 3).

Back to Paul in prison

Naturally, the apostle was thrilled to welcome a friend, but I imagine that his expression quickly changed to one of concern when he heard what his friend had to say. Certain people had arrived in his home church and were beginning to spread wrong teaching about the Lord Jesus Christ. What is more, this problem was not confined only to the believers who met in Colosse. The danger, which was menacing this congregation, was also threatening to cause disruption to every group of Christians who met throughout the region.

The person whom Paul received on that day was probably Epaphras. We know that Epaphras belonged to the Colossian church (4:12). Philemon, too, was almost certainly a member of the same church.

Many times Paul had faced opposition from the Jews, particularly, when new converts — who were not Jews — were received into the church without first being circumcised. (See some of the details of Paul's argument with Peter over this matter in Galatians 2:11-14.) But the disturbing news that Epaphras brought on that day was not just about Jewish resistance to Christianity. It was that false teaching about the Lord Jesus Christ was being widely taught. Certain people had come into the church who behaved as though they were much more spiritual than ordinary

Christians; they claimed to have 'superior' knowledge of sacred things. This may have been the beginnings of what later came to be known as Gnosticism.

However, we do not know what it is that Epaphras actually said to Paul. But what we can do is to read Paul's answers in the letter he wrote to the church at Colosse. So, as we study this letter, it will be like listening to one side of a telephone conversation. We can get some idea of what the person at the other end of the line is saying by the part of the conversation that we hear. However, Paul's answers tell us all that we need to know about the Christian faith and how we ought to live it.

On the one hand, the wrong teaching may have arisen among some Jews who were legalistic and who wanted to place great emphasis on human tradition (Colossians 2:8) and rules (Colossians 2:20-21). Or, on the other hand, it may have come from those who claimed to be 'in the know' (the Greek word *gnosis* means knowledge). This group taught that matter — anything that was physical or created — was evil and that only 'the spirit' was good. Because of this, they believed that it was impossible for God to be involved in creation. They taught that the world came into being through a complicated process by which some lesser god was responsible for its creation.

It would seem that the problem at Colosse was a combination of these two different strands of false teaching. What we do know is that when Paul replied to them his central theme was the supremacy of Christ.

SUMMARIZE IT

We have learned so far that Paul received disturbing news about the church at Colosse, probably from Epaphras, who was one of the members of the Colossian church. Teaching was being given that diverted the Christian believers away from the centrality of Christ.

PRACTICAL TASKS

When Paul's letter first arrived at Colosse, the church would have been gathered together to hear it read. Although it had various sections, it did not have the chapter and verse headings that we have in our Bibles; these were added much later. Like any other letter, it was written to be read right through, from beginning to end.

1. Make a note of every reference in the letter to the person and work of the Lord Jesus Christ.

2. Write a brief description of each of these references. Look especially at chapter 1:15-19 and at chapter 3:1-4.

QUESTION TIME

1. *The centrality of Christ in the life of the church and in the lives of individuals is emphasized.*

WORK AT IT

Why is this still a vital matter for Christians and churches today?

2. *In the days of the Colossian church, various other matters were being given equal status to Christ. What things are there in your own background that are seeking to have equal authority with Christ in your life?*

CHAPTER TWO

OPENING
GREETINGS

LOOK IT UP

BIBLE READING

Colossians 1:1-2

WHAT THE TEXT TEACHES

Sometimes we find letters that we have received long ago. Frequently these letters remind us of events that we have forgotten, and also of some we would rather not be reminded of because they bring to mind days that were difficult and sad.

When we read Paul's letter to the Colossians, we get some insight into the problems the believers were experiencing at that time. But, in addition, we can learn a great deal about the Christian faith and how we should live our lives today.

The author of this letter (1:1)

There is no doubt who wrote this letter. It starts in the characteristic way of all letters in Roman times with the name of the person who wrote it being the very first word. It begins with 'Paul'. Paul describes himself as 'an apostle'. He did not have to tell them what the implications of his office were. It would seem that there was no doubt in their minds about his apostleship, and the authority that that gave him from God (compare Galatians 1:1; 1 Corinthians 1:1 and 2 Corinthians 1:1).

In this introductory verse, Paul is merely pointing out that the Lord had sent him on a special mission with authority to proclaim the word of the Lord (compare, for example, Isaiah 61:1). The fact that he was an apostle was his 'badge of office'. Perhaps he needed to tell them what the role was that God had called him to fulfil because he had never visited the town or church of Colosse. He explained to them that he had not taken for himself the office of 'apostle'; he was 'an apostle of Christ Jesus *by the will of God'* (italics mine). Like his Master, he had not come to do his own will, but to carry out the desires of his Father in heaven (John 6:38).

It is highly likely that a number of the members of the Colossian church had heard Paul preach and teach. We know that two of them were active workers on his (and the Lord's) behalf: Epaphras and Philemon. But, perhaps, to give added weight to his letter, the apostle mentioned that Timothy, who was with him, agreed with all that he had written. Timothy, together with Epaphras and Philemon, was well known to the church at Colosse.

It is thought that the church at Colosse came into being during the two-year period when Paul had discussions in the lecture hall of Tyrannus (Acts 19:9-10). Luke tells us that 'all the Jews and Greeks who lived in the province of Asia heard the word of the Lord'. Of course, it is obvious that Luke means that large numbers of people in the whole area heard the gospel preached;

WORK IT OUT

he did not literally mean that every single man, woman and child learned of Christ's salvation during those years.

PRACTICAL TASKS

1. Think about the value of family relationships. Notice how Paul thinks in terms of a family relationship when he speaks about the fellowship of the church.

2. Look through this letter and note down each reference to members of the Christian family. How are they to conduct themselves one to another? (see 1:1; 1:12-13; 3:9; 3:13; 3:18-22; 4:7; 4:9; 4:10).

SUMMARIZE IT

We have learned so far that Paul wrote many letters to churches and individuals.

The recipients of this letter (1:2)

Paul describes the believers at Colosse as 'holy and faithful brothers in Christ at Colosse'. The fact that he called them 'brothers' does not mean that there were only men in the church in that town; nor is it saying that only the male members were of any value. Paul uses this word as a general term to denote a family; he means men and women, as well as boys and girls.

He calls them 'holy' not because they were more important than the other citizens of Colosse. He uses this term to explain that when they had been born again through Christ's cleansing blood, they were separated from the world around them. This does not mean that they behaved as though they were so important that they had nothing to do with their neighbours, for fear of being contaminated by them. It indicated that even though they were loyal citizens of Colosse, they were also living in a different kingdom: the kingdom of God. Through Christ's redemption, they had been separated from the contaminating influences of the world around them, and they had been 'set apart' for God's use and glory.

By calling them 'holy', Paul was not saying that they were to shut themselves away in a monastery or convent. In the negative sense, they sought to 'put to death' whatever belonged to their earthly nature (Paul explains the kinds of things he means in 3:5-9); and in the positive sense, they endeavoured to 'put on' Christ (see his exhortation in 3:10-14).

Paul also described the believers at Colosse as 'faithful brothers in Christ'. As they had been saved, they wanted to serve the Lord. When I was first converted as a teenager, preachers often used to remind Christian people that they had been 'saved to serve'. Christ has called his people out of darkness and into his wonderful light (1 Peter 2:9-10), not so that they can be 'so heavenly minded that they are of no earthly use'. He has called them so that they can work for him and for the extension of his kingdom.

Three times in this letter, Paul speaks of faithful brothers who worked with him and who were no doubt known to the Christians at Colosse. He says that Epaphras is 'a faithful minister of Christ' (1:7). Tychicus is 'a faithful minister and fellowservant in the Lord' (4:7) and Onesimus is 'our faithful and dear brother' (4:9). Each of these worked hard for the glory of God, and Paul uses the same term to describe the believers in the Colossian church. They had been loyal to the Christian message and had not deviated from the apostles teaching, but they had also worked hard to reach out with the gospel that was bearing fruit in their area as well as 'all over the world' (1:6).

To emphasize these things, Paul deliberately described God's people as being 'in Christ at Colosse'. This can be translated as 'in Christ, in Colosse'.

SUMMARIZE **IT**

We have seen so far that Paul did not write solely on his own authority. He was inspired by the Holy Spirit to write what would be beneficial to the church. To give

added weight to his letter, he involved Timothy
and he also mentioned respected members of the
Colossian church who would have been able to
allay any fears that anyone might have had about
Paul's authority.

The greetings he gives in this letter (1:2)

This is the usual greeting that Paul gave in most of his
letters. It combines the normal Roman greeting with
the Jewish one, except that he gave both of them a Christian overtone. 'Grace to you was a common greeting
between people living in the Roman world.'[1] But the
grace that Paul wrote about is that which is God's gra-
cious, unmerited gift; it is granted to each of his people
through the atoning sacrifice of Christ upon the cross
of Calvary. Grace is a very big word; it speaks of all of
the blessings of salvation — past, present and future
(notice the way in which Paul uses the word 'delivered'
in 2 Corinthians 1:10).

When Paul speaks about peace he does not mean an
absence of war and conflict. He is talking about the
'peace of God, which transcends all understanding'
(Philippians 4:7). This is a peace that sustains God's
people, even when they are going through great and
serious times of trial. The only people who can experi-
enco this peace are those who have found 'peace with
God' first of all, because they have been justified
through faith (Romans 5:1-2).

SUMMARIZE IT

We have noticed so far that the greetings that Paul gives are not merely put in his letter to obey the conventions of his day. They are there to show his spiritual concern that the recipients might know God's blessing in their lives.

In our next chapter (which comments on Colossians 1:3-7), we will take a closer look at the wonderful blessings that come to those who have faith in the Lord Jesus Christ.

QUESTION TIME

DISCUSS IT

1. 'In Christ', the Colossians believers were holy. They were holy because God had set them apart for his glory. The book of Leviticus emphasizes the fact that God is holy, but it also states that because of his holiness, we, too, should seek to live holy lives. Use some of the following texts to help you understand the implications of holy living: the book of Leviticus; 2 Corinthians 6:14-18; Romans 12:1-2; 1 Peter 1:13-16.

2. The Colossians are described as 'faithful brothers'. Read the parable of the talents in Matthew 25:14-30 and notice what the Lord

Jesus Christ says about those who are faithful to him. What needs to be altered in your life so that you can be more faithful to the Lord and his teachings?

THE GUIDE

CHAPTER THREE

THE EFFECTS
OF THE GOSPEL
MESSAGE

BIBLE READING

Colossians 1:3-8

WHAT THE TEXT TEACHES

A powerful note of thanksgiving always features near the beginning of Paul's letters. When he heard news of his friends at Colosse, he was filled with thanksgiving. He knew some of the members of the church personally and he had received good reports about the rapid spread of the gospel from that place. Notice that Paul includes Timothy and (probably) Epaphras in his thanksgiving for them and he tells them that he regularly gave thanks for all the believers. He says, 'We always thank God, the Father of our Lord Jesus Christ, when we pray for you' (italics mine).

Paul was always grateful for the care he had received from the Colossians. He naturally thanked them for their kindness, but his thanks were especially directed to God, but not to any god. He thanked the one who is 'the Father of our Lord Jesus Christ'. We can see from this that true prayer is never selfish. Although we sincerely thank God for his help and guidance, prayer should always rise above our circumstances and be focused on God from whom we received our salvation.

The fact that Paul emphasizes that God is the 'Father of our Lord Jesus Christ' reminds us that if we are truly born again, we are his children and we should delight in obeying his commands.

SUMMARIZE   IT

We have seen so far that Paul was thankful to God when he heard good news about the Colossian church. He wanted the believers to realize that they were not on their own; the relationship between Christians is one of mutual care and concern.

PRACTICAL TASKS

1. Make a list of the names of people for whom you can thank God because he has brought them into your circle of acquaintance, and they have been a blessing to you.

The blessings of the gospel

Paul always thanked God for all of those who had come to believe in the Lord Jesus Christ as their Saviour. He was especially grateful because the believers at Colosse were making good spiritual progress. He says, 'We [he means himself, Timothy, and the other Christians who

WHAT THE TEXT TEACHES

were with him] have heard of your faith in Christ Jesus and of the love you have for all the saints.'

It was their 'faith' he had heard about, but this 'faith' was not merely a statement of what they believed; it was faith in someone — Christ Jesus. The faith which they had in Christ was so rich that it was coupled with love for 'all the saints'. When Paul speaks about 'your faith in Christ Jesus', he is not placing the emphasis on their decision to believe in Christ; he is speaking about the personal relationship that they had with Christ because he had died to save them from their sins.

A church should consist of those who have truly come to faith in Christ and have received him as Lord and Saviour. But it should also be a fellowship which is characterized by love — not just love for lovely people, but for 'all the saints'. We are not told that we should be great friends with everyone in our church. That could be difficult if one or more of the members of our congregation had quite different temperaments from us. However, we are required to 'love' them. This is no easy task. But when we remember that Christ died for us, even though we were sinners, then we can accept the requirement that we should love all of those who have also been redeemed by the precious blood of Christ.

The source of these blessings is 'hope'. But this 'hope' is no vague ideal that may, or may

not, come to anything. The Christian's hope is something definite. It is 'stored up ... in heaven'. Peter speaks
of the same experience when he tells his readers that
'the God and Father of our Lord Jesus Christ ... has
given us new birth into a living hope [which is]... kept
in heaven for you' (1 Peter 1:3-4). Christians look forward to heaven; that is their hope. Yet this fact does
not mean that they do nothing except eagerly look forward to the day when they will be relieved of the pain
and toil of this life. The Christian's hope of heaven
enlarges his faith and love for all the saints in the
present.

The Old Testament prophets proclaimed their message as 'the word of the Lord'. Paul uses similar language to speak about the gospel; he calls it 'the word of
truth'. The believers rejoiced because they had heard
'the word of truth'. They had not experienced the blessings of salvation because of something they, or some
other man or woman, had done. A message which had
been preached had reached their ears and they had
gladly responded to it in repentance and faith. Paul calls
it the 'word of truth' because it is nothing less than the
truth about man and his sin, and Christ and his atoning
death on the cross.

SUMMARIZE IT

We have learned so far that Christians have faith
and love for their Lord and for one another. These

blessings spring from the hope of eternal life. The message has been received by the preaching of the 'word of truth'.

The spread of the gospel

The believers had not kept the good news to themselves. They had passed the 'word of truth' on to others with great enthusiasm, so much so that the message of salvation was growing; it was behaving like a lush, healthy plant; it was growing and 'bearing fruit'.

Paul did not literally mean that the gospel was spreading to every country in the world; he was referring to the then known world. This was a statement to indicate the rapid spread of the gospel and its triumphant progress.

Paul speaks about the spread of the gospel in two ways. He says that the gospel was 'bearing fruit'. This may not necessarily mean that an increasingly large number of people were coming to faith in Christ. It does mean that those who did believe were being enriched in every part of their lives; they were seeing evidence of the fruit of the Spirit in their lives. But Paul also specifically mentions that the gospel was 'growing'. He means that more and more people were being brought out of the dominion of darkness, and into the kingdom of the Son (1:13).

WHAT THE TEXT TEACHES

PRACTICAL TASKS

1. Study Galatians 5:22-23. Notice that these 'fruits' are not necessarily to do with a physical increase, they are all related to spiritual (inward) growth. Compare these verses with Matthew 7:16-20, where Jesus speaks of good fruit and bad fruit.

2. Look up some of the 'growth' parables of Jesus and note down their main purpose (read Matthew 13:31-35).

3. Read the parable of the sower and the explanation Jesus gives in Matthew 13:1-23. Make a list of the things that try to prevent the spread of the gospel today where you live.

The Colossians 'understood God's grace in all its truth' (v. 6) because Epaphras had clearly explained it to them. They knew that grace is God's undeserved favour towards sinful men and women. Paul endorses Epaphras's work and is confident that he had taught the Colossians, and that they had understood his teaching. He knew this because the Holy Spirit was evidently at work in their lives; they displayed 'love in the Spirit' (v. 8).

This love was not mere friendship, nor the kind of love that is found within a family. It was much more than fellowship between people who are thrown together in a club or society. It was love in the Spirit. R.C. Lucas says, 'There could be no surer sign of their living faith and expectant hope than this' (compare 1 Corinthians 13:1-3). [1] The spiritual love which they displayed was a certain indication that God had sent his one and only Son, and he was dwelling in them and in their church fellowship (1 John 4:9). Their love was a response to and a reflection of the love of God.

QUESTION TIME

DISCUSS IT

1. Examine each of the following verses in the letter to the Colossians: 1:12; 2:7; 3:15,17; and 4:2. For what does Paul give thanks? How can the church demonstrate thanksgiving more effectively today? What can individual Christians do to be more thankful, and how can they encourage their fellow-believers to be more grateful for the blessings they have received?

2. Look up the following passages where 'faith, love and hope' appear: Romans 5:2-5; 1 Corinthians 13:13; Galatians 5:5-6; 1 Thessalonians 3; 5:8; and Hebrews 10:22-24. Using these texts, discuss some practical measures that can be taken to point people away from a loveless, faithless and hopeless society and towards Christ.

3. Notice the effect of faith, love and hope in the Thessalonian church (1 Thessalonians 1:3) and compare this with the words of Jesus to the much more mature church at Ephesus in Revelation 2:1. What made the difference to the ministry of the Thessalonians?

4. *How would you answer someone who said to you, 'You are only a Christian because you want to go to heaven when you die.' Show how your Christian faith has relevance to this life, as well as to the next.*

CHAPTER FOUR

SPIRITUAL
PRAYER

LOOK IT UP

BIBLE READING

Colossians 1:9-14

WHAT THE TEXT TEACHES

Prayer is fundamental to the life of a Christian. Yet it is the most difficult and most neglected of all Christian duties. It is, however, the most blessed activity in which God's people can engage. There is an old hymn which says that 'Prayer is the Christian's vital breath, the Christian's native air'.[1]

One of Paul's beautiful prayers is found in this section of the letter to the Colossians. The reason he prayed for the believers at Colosse at that time was because Epaphras had told him about their progress in the Christian life (1:7). This is why he writes, 'Since the day we heard about you, we have not stopped praying for you.' Notice how Paul speaks about prayer here. He says that he prays for the Colossians and he also asks God for certain things for them (1:9). It is instructive to make a list of each of the things he mentions in the verses we are studying.

You will notice that Paul's prayer list is very rich. He does not confine himself to minor matters, nor is he over concerned about the material needs of the people. Instead, he asks the Lord for spiritual blessings. He pleads with the Lord to 'fill [them] with the knowledge of his will through all spiritual wisdom and understanding'. In chapter 4:2 he is going to urge them to 'devote' themselves to prayer. Here, in this section, he demonstrates that he practises what he preaches.

It would seem that the false teachers who had come among them had told them that the teaching they had heard from Paul, and also that which had been relayed through Epaphras, was not noble enough. Instead, these false teachers urged the Colossians to follow their instructions and had promised them that, as a result, they would experience 'a fulness' that they never dreamed would be possible. This fulness seems to have centred on a 'knowledge' and 'power' that was far greater than anything they had come across before.

Notice how Paul handles this situation. He does not say, 'Don't listen to these wicked men, instead follow us.' He prays for these Christians that they would be '[*filled*] with the knowledge of [God's] will through all spiritual wisdom and understanding' (italics mine). This would come to them not through those who taught the mystical thinking which was emerging at that time. It would be taught by those faithful workers who passed on 'the apostle's teaching' which had been given in the days following the day of Pentecost (see Acts 2:42). This had been taught by Jesus to his disciples during his earthly life, and had been amplified during the period of forty days after his resurrection when he spoke to them 'about the kingdom of God' (Acts 1:3). However,

WHAT THE TEXT TEACHES

this teaching was not merely reserved for those who were extra special Christians; it was the right and privilege of everyone who had been 'rescued ... from the dominion of darkness and brought ... into the kingdom of the Son [God] loves' (Colossians 1:13).

When someone truly becomes a Christian, that person is 'justified freely by [God's] grace through the redemption that came by Christ Jesus' (Romans 3:24). As a believer grows in spiritual understanding and experience, he does not become more justified than he was previously. Those who are rescued from the dominion of darkness (i.e., their sin) are brought into God's kingdom at the moment of their conversion. It is not possible for someone to be 'half saved'. All of the way through the Bible, a distinction is made between the godly and ungodly, the saved and the unsaved. Salvation is a once-for-all event. A person is either saved or lost. Salvation is not by half measure.

Having said that, Christians must not stagnate; we must all grow in the Christian life; we must make progress. Each one must be 'eager to make [his or her] calling and election sure' (2 Peter 1:10). As we mediate upon the wonders of God's grace to us, we, who are but poor, feeble sinners, will rejoice at his grace in rescuing us from the 'dominion' of Satan's darkness. Praising God for these unmerited and generous blessings will

ensure that we become more mature and more effective in our Christian life and witness.

SUMMARIZE IT

We have seen so far how Paul prays that the
Colossian believers would be filled with the
knowledge of God's will, not because false
teachers had shown them a 'better way' but because the Lord had revealed his will to them.
God's 'filling' and 'power' granted to believers will
enable them to live a life worthy of the Lord.

PRACTICAL TASKS

1. Look up 1 Chronicles 22:12 and find out the two special
   attributes that David asks God to give to his son Solomon.
   Then look up 2 Chronicles 1:10 and notice the two things
   that Solomon asks God for as he begins his reign.

2. Read Psalm 1 and write down the differences between the
   godly and the ungodly person.

The 'religious visitors' at Colosse apparently wanted
to display their super-spirituality so that they would
gain more followers to themselves. However, Paul's aim
in seeing the believers '[filled] with the knowledge of
[God's] will' was so that they might live in a manner
worthy of the gospel. Pleasing God should be the aim

of every true Christian, not merely following a good teacher. Paul was not concerned to win people over to his way of thinking; he wanted to see them following the Lord and doing his will.

Paul lists some of the ways in which they should live a worthy life. They were to seek to please God in everything they did. They were to engage in good works so that they and others might glorify God; Paul calls this 'bearing fruit'. They were to become more mature in their knowledge of God and his ways (1:10). They were to be strengthened by God's glorious might (v. 11). This glorious might had been demonstrated in the Old Testament as God's 'right hand ... [which had] shattered the enemy' — that is, Egypt's power (Exodus 15:6). This same glorious might was to be made accessible to these Colossian Christians; and this should result in their having great endurance, patience and joy (1:11).

Paul uses two words that are translated as 'endurance' and 'patience' in English. Those who endure in their Christian lives persevere despite all difficulties. To live in such a way requires much patience, especially when dealing with difficult people. Notice that both words are used in the list of qualities of a servant of Christ in 2 Corinthians 6:4-6. We discover the qualities of a patient man in Proverbs 16:32. The quality of 'perseverance' (i.e., endurance) is praised in the church at Ephesus (Revelation 2:2-3).

'Joy' is one of the keynotes in Paul's letter to the Philippians. Throughout that letter Paul speaks of his joy (see especially Philippians 1:25; 2:2; 4:1).

Because of all God's blessings in the created realm, in the provision of our needs and in our salvation, we should be eager to thank God. The Christian who is '[filled] with the knowledge of [God's] will' will thank him from a joyful heart; there will be no grudging word of thanks for these things. Even the unsaved person experiences many blessings from God, for example, the blessings of nature, which include the gift of life itself. But the Christian has so much more for which to thank God.

The false teaching that was being given, in contradiction to the teaching of the apostles, may well have caused the young believers at Colosse to think that they were disqualified from entering into God's blessing. However, Paul makes it very clear that they were qualified to 'share in the inheritance of the saints in the kingdom of light'. In the Old Testament, God's people were promised that they would inherit the Promised Land and enjoy the blessings of God's reign. New Testament believers enjoy the promise of an 'inheritance that can never perish, spoil or fade' (1 Peter 1:4). In Canaan, there was much warfare and unhappiness. In God's kingdom, the kingdom of light there is no need of a 'lamp or the light of the sun' because 'the Lord God will give ... light' (Revelation 22:6).

Before people are saved, they are in darkness; they are lost in sin and degradation. When they become Christians, they are brought into God's kingdom and given the blessings of redemption and the forgiveness of sins.

In Exodus 21:8 we have God's rules for the redemption (i.e., the buying back) of a daughter who is sold as a servant. Israel was redeemed from the power of slavery in Egypt (Exodus 15:13). The bondage of slavery is likened to the hold that sin has over unsaved people. The blessings of salvation are made available to those whose sins have been forgiven through Christ's shed blood (see 1 Peter 1:18). Jesus speaks a great deal about the kingdom of God. In Matthew he calls this 'the kingdom of heaven'. The Lord taught the people about God's reign, and the willing obedience of the subjects of his kingdom (see Matthew 6:33; 1 Corinthians 6:9; 1 Thessalonians 2:12; 2 Thessalonians 1:5).

There are many pictures in the Bible that illustrate the stranglehold that sin has over people. Their rescue from such dominion shows the contrast between those who are in darkness and those who have been brought into the light. Notice this contrast in Psalm 40:1-3 and the difference brought about through this man's rescue. Psalm 66:1-7 shows us how God displays his powerful rule.

SUMMARIZE IT

We have seen so far that God's people should be thankful because he has qualified them, through the merits of his Son, to share in the inheritance of the saints, because they have been rescued from sin and brought into his kingdom through redemption and the forgiveness of their sins.

QUESTION TIME

1. *From the passage we are studying in this chapter, what are the true marks of a believer?*

2. *What did Jesus say about good works in Matthew 5:15-16? What is it that Jesus says will prevent our good works from having an effect? What does he say the result of our good works will be if we do as he says?*

CHAPTER FIVE

THE
SUPREMACY
OF CHRIST

THE **G** U I D E

BIBLE READING

Colossians 1:15-20

WHAT THE TEXT TEACHES

We now come to the heart of the matter that Paul wishes to bring to the attention of the Colossian church. The greetings and introductions have been completed and so Paul moves straight to this great passage in which he tells them about Christ and his authority and power.

The false teachers taught great error about Christ: instead of placing him as the centre of everything, they were drawing attention to them-selves and their 'great spiritual insights'. Paul acted differently. He did not wish to boast about his spiritually (see Philippians 3:7-8). Instead, he constantly pointed people to Christ and the cross.

Christ as supreme over all creation (1:15-17)

Paul tells us that '[Christ] is the image of the invisible God' and he is the 'firstborn over all creation'. This means that the whole of creation owes its existence to Christ. It is as though Paul were saying to the Colossians, 'Take no notice of those false teachers who are telling you that Christ is a mere manifestation of God — a spiritual force. He is 'the image of ... God'. In fact, he is God himself who came down to earth in human form.

The English word 'image' comes from the Greek word 'icon'. In Orthodox churches, there are icons of the saints (in the same way that there are icons on a computer screen). These icons represent the true object. But the Lord Jesus Christ is much greater than a lovely picture of God; he *is* God. Hebrews 1:3 explains this in more detail. There he is described as 'the radiance of God's glory and the *exact* representation of his being' (italics mine).

Because he created all things, he was before all things; he was 'with God' in the very beginning of all things (John 1:1 and see Genesis 1:1). The false teachers had obviously been telling the Colossians that Jesus was just one of the manifestations of the true God. But in these verses, Paul makes it abundantly clear that 'the Son [God] loves' (1:13) is nothing other than the 'image of the invisible God'.

Paul describes the Lord Jesus as 'the firstborn over all creation'. This does not mean he was the first person to be born. Jehovah's Witnesses and others who are in error at this point teach that he was the first being to be created. But the Scriptures tell us that he has existed from all eternity. In John 8:58 Jesus says, 'Before Abraham was born, I am!' The apostle evidently described the Lord Jesus as the firstborn because he holds the highest place in heaven and on earth.

The apostle then proceeds to list those powers that seem to have frightened and overawed the people of his day. He speaks of 'things in heaven and on earth'; things which are 'visible and invisible'; 'thrones or powers', 'rulers or authorities'. He insists that it is by Christ that each one of these things has been created. This means that any power or authority that they possessed was entirely dependent on Christ, the Lord.

PRACTICAL TASKS

1. Read verses 15–20 of Colossians chapter 1 and make note of each time the word 'all' occurs. Paul mostly writes 'all things', but once he speaks of 'all creation' and in verse 19 he says, 'all his fulness'.

2. Write down the names of as many things that you can think of that form part of the universe, for example, the stars, planet earth and the animal life that is found in and on the earth. Then include some of the microscopic things like rock crystals and tiny insects. Mediate on the vastness of creation — all that God, in Christ, has made out of nothing.

3. Find out, from an encyclopaedia or any reference book, how the planets revolve around the sun in an orderly way and how they all act in accordance with a God-given timetable.

4. Read Genesis 1:1 and compare it with John 1:1. Notice how, at the creation of the world, the Lord

WORK AT IT

Jesus (the Word) was already with the Father at, or before, the beginning of all things.

5. Read Exodus 4:22 and Psalm 89:27 and notice the use of the word 'firstborn'. This refers to the exalted position of Israel rather than its being the first (in chronological order) to be born.

SUMMARIZE IT

We have learned so far that through Christ the whole of creation has been made out of nothing. He not only made the heavens and the earth, but also holds it all together by his power.

Genesis 1:1 tells us that 'in the beginning God created the heavens and the earth', and Paul says, 'By him [that is, Jesus] all things were created.' This means that Jesus is God. Together with the Holy Spirit, these three persons form the Godhead. The rest of verse 15 and verse 16 explain that Christ not only created all things, but 'in him' alone do all things have meaning and purpose. Verse 17 tells us that 'he is before all things' and 'in him all things hold together'. A scientist will explain the tremendous power that is holding the smallest atom in place. Without this great force, everything would fly apart.

Verse 16 mentions all kinds of heavenly powers and intermediaries; these were the kind of 'beings' that fascinated and frightened the people of Paul's day. Since

Christ is Lord of creation, no true Christian (who would be 'in Christ') need fear any of these 'beings', because any existence and power they have is entirely dependent upon Christ.[1] There is nothing that these 'beings' can do to help us — it is useless to pray to them — nor can they harm us in any way because Christ is able to supply all of our needs. R. C. Lucas helpfully comments, 'How strange if he who is sufficient to sustain a universe, should be insufficient in power for the little church at Colosse'.[2]

SUMMARIZE IT

We have learned so far that no believer need fear unseen powers of evil because Christ is 'far above all rule' (Ephesians 1:21-22).

Christ is supreme in the church (1:18-20)

No man (Pope or Metropolitan) or any reigning monarch is head of the church; Christ holds that distinction. In describing the church as a human body, Paul is causing us to observe the role of the head in relation to the body. A human being can exist without an arm or leg, but if his or her head is cut off then the brain, the driving power of the whole system, is removed. As head of the church, Christ is the beginning (at creation) and the firstborn (see verse 15) from among the dead. There were cases in the Old and in the New Testament where people had been raised to life from the dead, but each of these people eventually died for the second time. Jesus Christ was the first person to be raised from the dead, never to die again (Acts 26:23). This means that he is not only supreme in all creation, but he is also foremost over everything that exists, including 'the church of the firstborn' (Hebrews 12:23).

PRACTICAL TASKS

1. Look up Ephesians 1:22-23 and 1 Corinthians 12:27. Write a short description of Christ as head of the church.

2. The following scripture references give details of some of the people who were raised to life after they had died: 2 Kings 4:35; Luke 7:15; John 11:44; Acts 9:36-41 and Acts 20:7-11. Look up each of these references and write a sentence or two about each one of them. Note that every one of these people eventually died again.

3. Christ rose from the dead as 'the firstfruits of those who have fallen asleep' (1 Corinthians 15:20). Unlike the others who came back to life but died a second time, Christ is alive for evermore (Hebrews 7:25). He is the 'firstfruits' not only because he is the most important person to come back to life, but also because his people have been 'raised with Christ' (Colossians 3:1).

WHAT THE TEXT TEACHES

Verse 19 tells us of the pleasure God had in ensuring that 'all his fulness' dwelt in Christ. This shows us that the Lord Jesus was obviously not some distant emanation of the Godhead. John 1:14 explains that 'the Word [Christ] became flesh and made his dwelling among us'. This statement would have taken the thoughts of Paul's Jewish readers back to the time when their forefathers wandered through the desert on their journey from Egypt to the Promised Land. Just as they dwelt in tents at that time and God himself dwelt at the centre of the tabernacle (tent) they erected in the desert, so also the Lord Christ dwells with his people today.

There is much disharmony and strife in the world today, just as there was in Paul's day. Reconciliation both between individuals and nations is greatly needed. Verse 20 tells us that reconciliation is a work which God has performed. Through Christ, 'he reconciles all things to himself'. There is no need to wait till the end of time. Peace has already been made through the death of Christ upon the cross. The heart of the Christian message is 'Christ and him crucified' (1 Corinthians 2:1-5). True believers have been saved through the atoning blood of Christ shed for repentant sinners. No true, lasting peace can come merely through the powerful words of those who, like the false teachers at Colosse, fail to put the cross at the centre of their preaching.

THE SUPREMACY OF CHRIST

The Lord Jesus Christ, who is both God and man, brought peace to this sinful world through his death on the cross.

SUMMARIZE IT

We have learned so far that Christ is the head of the church, and he has all the authority of God as well as his presence with him. He has brought peace through his sacrificial death on the cross.

QUESTION TIME

1. What does John 1:15-18 and Hebrews 1:2-4 teach us about the Lord Jesus Christ?

2. How is the power of Christ in creation demonstrated in Colossians 1:15-17?

3. 1 Corinthians 15:20 speaks of Christ's resurrection as the 'firstfruits of those who have fallen asleep'. God has made true Christian believers 'alive with Christ' (Colossians 2:13). How does the reality of this truth affect your life today?

4. What evidence is there that God dwells with his people today? The following references will help you to answer this question: Psalm 27:5; Psalm 68:5; Psalm 90:1; Ezekiel 37:26-27; Revelation 21:3.

5. *What has Christ's death achieved for his people?*
   (See Exodus 12:13; Luke 2:14; Ephesians 2:13;
   Romans 5:19; Hebrews 9:22; 1 Peter 1:18-19).

THE GUIDE

CHAPTER SIX

THE EFFECTS
OF CHRIST'S
SHED BLOOD

LOOK IT UP

Colossians 1:21-23

WHAT THE TEXT TEACHES

Karl Marx wrote a great deal about alienation. He said that mankind has been alienated because of the power of capitalism.[1] However, centuries before Marx was born, the apostle Paul wrote about the alienation that mankind has suffered which is not the result of capitalism, but sin.

In these three verses, Paul starts to apply the teaching that he has been giving about the person and work of the Lord Jesus Christ to individual Christians; he uses the words 'you' and 'your' eight times in these three verses. He refers to the past — 'once [before you were born again] *you were alienated* from God' (1:21, italics mine). In the next verse, he speaks about their present experience: '*He has reconciled you*' (1:22, italics mine); and then he speaks about the future. He tells them that they will continue to experience the blessings of freedom from the power of sin, '*if you continue in your faith*' (1:23, italics mine). You will have noted this teaching in your answer to question 5 at the end of the previous chapter.

Paul also used the word 'you' to emphasize to these Gentile believers that his words applied to them. It was to point out that those, whom the Jews considered to be 'far away' from 'citizenship in Israel', had also been 'brought near through the blood of Christ' (see Ephesians 2:11-13).

A person's state without Christ (1:21)

The apostle starts by outlining the state and condition of people before they become Christians: 'Once you were alienated from God.' By this he means that they were not only cut off from the spiritual blessings of God, but that they were actually enemies of God. This fact had been demonstrated by their behaviour, which Paul describes by using the shocking word 'evil'. As always, Paul recognized that evil behaviour begins in the mind.

Evil deeds are conceived because we have a strong desire to do something which is wrong. Then we start thinking about the thing that we desire to do, and unless these thoughts are checked, we find that we are led to indulge our sinful desires. This, in turn, leads to wrong actions. The person who steals something from a shop has, first of all, had a desire to obtain the object he or she sees. Then the thought process starts, and this builds up into a plan to steal it. Paul was well aware of this process in the hearts and minds of sinners, and this is why he often connects the heart and the mind (Philippians 4:7 and Ephesians 4:18).

WHAT THE TEXT TEACHES

What has been achieved through Christ's death? (1:22)

The apostle's thoughts are still centred on what was achieved by Christ when he shed his blood on the cross (1:20). The unsaved person is alienated from God because of his sin; he is an enemy of all godliness. There can be no peace when his thoughts are given over to hatred and evil behaviour. This means that there can only be enmity between such a person and God. Only those who have 'clean hands and a pure heart' can stand in God's holy place (Psalm 24:4) because God's eyes are 'too pure to look on evil' (Habbakkuk 1:13). Not only are people free from blemish, through Christ's righteousness being transferred to them (2 Corinthians 5:21), but they are also free from accusation. The apostle tells the Romans that 'there is now no condemnation for those who are in Christ Jesus' (Romans 8:1).

It took the death of a pure and blameless human being, who gave up his life to pay the price for such sin, to bring about reconciliation. Christ is the only person who fits this description. Because he is fully man and fully God, he meets our need of reconciliation with God (Hebrews 7:26). Through his death on the cross, he has brought about reconciliation between the believer and God, who is holy.

Paul speaks about Christ's physical body because he needs to establish that Christ was, and is, both God and man. For the Gnostics, it would have been quite impossible to think of Christ as having a body. Certainly, they could not conceive of him being 'the firstborn from among the dead' (Colossians 1:18). Yet John, the apostle, speaks of Jesus' life 'which was from the beginning, which we have heard, which we have seen with our eyes, which we have looked at and our hands have touched', and he says that he has 'appeared'. (1 John 1:1-2). Also, Peter was not following 'cleverly invented stories' when he told the people about the 'power and coming of our Lord Jesus Christ'. Instead, he was one of the eye-witnesses of 'his majesty' (2 Peter 1:16).

What will be achieved through the death of Christ?

The word 'if' at the beginning of verse 23 does not suggest that there is any doubt in Paul's mind about the efficacy of the gospel to save people. He is merely emphasizing the need for God's people to continue in the faith. There should never be any thought in a believer's mind that once he has come to the cross of Christ and been saved, he can then relax.

PRACTICAL TASKS

1. Read the following verses and heed the warnings against complacency. The ancient Israelites refused to change their

ways and so were taken away into exile, never to
the return (Amos 6:1 and Zephaniah 1:12).

2. Note how Paul uses the word 'if' in Philippians 2:1.
   See that there is no doubt in his mind about the
   spiritual benefits of being united to Christ.

WHAT THE TEXT TEACHES

Those who continue in the faith (i.e., the truth
of the gospel) will realize the need to keep building upon it. Their trust in Christ must be estab-
lished and firm. The 'house' of their faith must
be built on the rock which is Christ. Various
storms will blow upon 'the household of faith',
seeking to topple it. The false teaching, which
was being brought by those who were troubling
the church at Colosse, is an example of the wind
of wrong doctrine which can cause havoc to any
Christian or in the church. This is why Paul urges
the believers not to be 'moved from the hope held
out in the gospel' (1:23). The hope of future blessing should be their goal. They must not be
tempted to think that these new teachers could
give them spiritual 'knowledge' which would
bring them greater blessings than the pure message of the gospel that they had heard through
Epaphras and other preachers.

This gospel was bearing fruit all over the
world (1:6) and Paul was a servant of the gospel.
It was his task to give himself to proclaiming it
to every creature under heaven.

QUESTION TIME

1. *Paul tells the Philippians about the peace of God (4:7). What does God's peace guard and how does it do that? Study Philippians 4:4-6 and make a list of some of the ways in which believers can be sure to experience the peace of God.*

2. *Notice how Jesus described the house built on a rock in Matthew 7:24-28, and remember that Christ is the immovable rock on which God's people are built (Psalm 18:2; 40:2; 1 Corinthians 10:4 and 1 Peter 2:8). Also observe that the Galatians had quickly moved away from the true gospel (Galatians 1:6, compare 1 Corinthians 15:58). In view of these things, how can a church or individual Christian withstand the destructive effects of the fierce storms of evil doctrine? (Ephesians 4:14-15).*

THE GUIDE

CHAPTER SEVEN

PAUL'S WORK AS A SERVANT

LOOK IT UP

BIBLE READING

Colossians 1:24-29

WHAT THE TEXT TEACHES

All of Paul's energy was taken up with the Lord Jesus Christ. He wanted to ensure that his friends at Colosse, and elsewhere, put the Lord first in their lives — that is, in their thinking, planning and actions. Because of this, he did not want to draw attention to himself or his achievements. He knew that God's people are required to 'walk humbly with [their] God' (Micah 6:8); they must not be concerned to promote themselves, or their own ideas.

However, in this passage Paul does speak about himself and his desires. These are not selfish desires; he is not seeking to receive praise from people. He is rejoicing because of the things that he suffered for the believers. He then says something which sounds very strange to our ears. He says, 'I fill up in my flesh what is still lacking in regard to Christ's afflictions.' It is clear that he does not mean that through his suffering, he is adding to the work of redemption which Christ wrought on the cross for the salvation of his people. That would be quite contrary to his other

teaching (Colossians 1:20, for example). On the cross
Christ declared, 'It is finished' (John 19:30) — that is,
the work of redemption has been completed.

What Paul is discussing is the requirement for Christians to suffer for the sake of Christ. When he was saved
on the Damascus road, God said to Ananias, 'I will show
him [Paul] how much he must suffer for my name' (Acts
9:16). Paul certainly went on to suffer many things and
they were all for 'the sake of [Christ's] body, which is
the church'.

There is no doubt that suffering is the lot of God's
people. In the task of spreading the gospel, Christians
are required to work at it with such diligence that they
are to be like soldiers and 'endure hardship' (2 Timothy 2:3). The church, which suffers for Christ's sake,
grows stronger as a result. We can see the effects of
Paul's suffering in 2 Corinthians 11:23-28; 12:9; 1:7 and
Philippians 3:10. These passages tell us some of the
blessings which come to God's people when they suffer
for the sake of Christ.

SUMMARIZE IT

We have seen so far that Christians must be
humble people who do not draw attention to
themselves; however, they are required to suffer
for the sake of Christ. Any 'glory' that comes from
their self-sacrifice must be directed to the honour
of Christ alone.

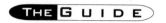

Paul's commission

Rather than encouraging church members to praise him, Paul reminds the Colossians that he is their servant —that is, their slave. God has commissioned him to do this work. In an army, the commissioned officers are required to obey immediately and explicitly the instructions given to them by the commanding General. In the same way, Paul was acting under the instructions of the Lord.

He is not the servant of the churches, required to do what they say, nor to make it his main aim to please them. He has been commissioned by God to present to the people 'the word of God in its fulness' (Colossians 1:25).

He describes the gospel as 'the mystery'. To describe the secret information that was only available to an exclusive group of people, pagans used this word 'mystery'. This is why Paul carefully chooses this word, but he goes on to explain that, in the gospel, that which '[had] been kept hidden for ages and generations' has now been disclosed to the saints. This mystery is glorious and is 'Christ in you [Gentile and Jewish believers], the hope of glory.'

In the past, only the Jews had caught a glimpse of these blessings, but now God had chosen to 'make known' his glorious riches, even to 'the

WHAT THE TEXT TEACHES

Gentiles'. Formerly these were 'excluded from citizen-ship in Israel and foreigners to the covenants of the promise... But now in Christ Jesus [those] who once were far away have been brought near through the blood of Christ' (Ephesians 2:12-13).

PRACTICAL TASKS

1. Trace Paul's use of the word 'mystery' through the New Testament and notice that it means 'a truth which was once hidden but is now revealed' (see Romans 11:25; 16:25; 1 Corinthians 15:51; Ephesians 1:9; 3:3-9; 5:32; 6:19; Colossians 1:26-27; 2:2; 4:3; and 1 Timothy 3:16).

2. Notice how the Bible uses the word 'glory' frequently of a bright light (see Luke 2:9; Acts 22:11; 1 Corinthians 15:41, AV and 2 Corinthians 3:7-8).

3. Notice how the New Testament speaks about the riches of the gospel of God's grace (see Colossians 2:2; Ephesians 1:7,18; 3:8,16).

SUMMARIZE IT

We have seen so far that what was hidden before the gospel era has now been revealed to those who are 'in Christ'. This is the glory of Christ and the riches of the gospel.

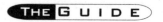

The work of preachers of the gospel

While pastors of necessity become involved in all kinds of work outside of their own congregation, they must remember that their chief task is to 'proclaim him' — that is, Christ. This is not just to preach powerful sermons which please the hearers, it is to '[admonish] and [teach] everyone with all wisdom'. These twin tasks are outlined by Paul in his farewell address to the elders at Ephesus in Acts 20:20-21. There he says that he has 'not hesitated to preach anything that would be helpful ... but [has] taught ... publicly and from house to house. I have declared to both Jews and Greeks that they must turn to God in repentance and have faith in our Lord Jesus.'

To counter the intellectual exclusiveness of the Gnostic teachers in Colosse, Paul emphasizes that this gospel is for 'everyone'. He uses this word twice in verse 28 of Colossians chapter 1. This is to emphasize the universal nature of the gospel. He is not saying that everyone will be saved, but that this good news is for everyone, Jew and Gentile alike — that is, everyone who will turn from his or her sin and come to Christ in faith.

Paul's whole energy is devoted to admonishing and teaching everyone who will listen in order that they may be presented to God 'perfect'.

WHAT THE TEXT TEACHES

It seems that 'perfect' was another word used by the false teachers at Colosse. Paul uses it here to mean mature. He wanted them all to be active in pursuing Christ so that they all would reach maturity in the faith.

SUMMARIZE IT

We have seen so far that the aim of the servant of Christ is to preach Christ. This is a task which demands much energy, but the power of Christ works through those who seek to 'admonish' and 'teach' believers so that they will one day be presented to Christ as part of his perfect church.

QUESTION TIME

1. What should be the character and work of someone who has been commissioned by God to preach the gospel? (See 1 Corinthians 4:1-2; Titus 1:7 and 1 Peter 4:10.)

2. How can sinful men and women become perfect? (See Matthew 5:48; Ephesians 5:25-27; Leviticus 19:2).

3. Why do many Christians in these days not devote themselves to working hard to preach Christ, as the believers did in New Testament times? (See 1 Thessalonians 2:9; 1 Corinthians 4:12-13.)

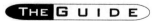

4. Why was Paul actively engaged in following his Master's commission? *(1 Thessalonians 2:19-20; 5:23; 1 Corinthians 15:10; Ephesians 3:7).*

CHAPTER EIGHT

PAUL'S MANY CONCERNS

BIBLE READING

Colossians 2:1-5

WHAT THE TEXT TEACHES

In this passage, Paul continues in the same personal vein. When we hear of trouble coming upon close friends, we do everything in our power to help them. We do not mind what sacrifice or financial cost we have to bear, so long as we can help them get out of trouble. That is natural. But would we go to such lengths for strangers? Paul did. Obviously, nobody would expect him to be so concerned about people he did not know personally. This is why he says to the Colossians, 'I want you to know how much I am struggling for you.' He was not boasting. He was merely saying, 'Although I have never visited you and I do not know many of you, that does not mean that I will not do all in my power to help you.'

He writes about 'you' — that is, the church at Colosse, then he speaks of a second group, 'those at Laodicea', and finally a third group, 'all who have not met me personally'. Who is this third group of people? It would seem that they were from another church. From chapter 4:13 we see that Epaphras (who came from Colosse) had dealings with a group at Hierapolis. A glance at a map of the region will show that these three churches (i.e., groups of believers who were organized in Christian fellowships) were all fairly close to one another. This means that false teachers could have influenced all of these churches, and the advice Paul had to give therefore applied to all of them. However, as Paul addressed his letter to the Colossians, it was perhaps this church that was the one that was in the greatest danger. Even so, he wanted this letter to be passed on to the Laodicean church, so that that church could read it and the one (which has been lost) that Paul wrote to the Laodiceans, he wanted the Colossian church to read (see Colossians 4:16).

In chapter 1:29, the apostle had spoken about '*labour, struggling* with all [Christ's] *energy*, which so *powerfully works* in me' (italics mine). This verse is full of words that express great effort. Here, in chapter 2:1, Paul again uses the word 'struggling'. The Greek word for this is the one from which we get the English word 'agony'.

Paul's purpose

As always, Paul's concern was not for himself, but for the welfare of God's people. He wanted to encourage them in heart and also to know that they were united in love. A lack of love among God's people is one of the first signs of spiritual declension. Quite obviously the new teachers, with their emphasis on the superiority of those who had special knowledge, were in danger of causing divisions among the believers. But Paul wanted to point out that one of the main ways in which Christian people can gain 'full riches of complete understanding' is to be overflowing with love for Christ, for their fellow-believers and also for the unsaved around them. True Christian love is seen in Christ who 'loved the church and gave himself up for her' (Ephesians 5:25).

PRACTICAL TASKS

1. Note the various areas of Christian endeavour where believers are called upon to struggle (see Romans 15:30; Ephesians 6:12; Philippians 1:29-30 and Hebrews 12:4).

2. Look up what Jesus had to say about the need for his people to love one another (see John 13:1-35 and John 15:1-19).

SUMMARIZE IT

We have seen so far that Paul's concern was not just for those he knew personally, but for all of God's people, especially those who were in danger of being led astray by false

WORK AT IT

teaching. He wanted to encourage them to have love for Christ and for one another.

Combating 'fine-sounding' arguments

Most of us are fearful of having to challenge those who teach false doctrines. These people often know their teaching extremely well and have even studied biblical literature to the point that they are sufficiently skilled to contest its assertions. How, then, can ordinary Christians witness to their faith when speaking to such educated people?

Paul's desire was that the Colossians should seek to have 'complete understanding, in order that they [would] know the mystery of God, namely, Christ, in whom are hidden all the treasures of wisdom and knowledge' (2:2-3). He wanted God's people to work hard at studying the Scriptures because only through a deep knowledge of the teaching and meaning of the Bible can anyone withstand the power of the 'fine-sounding' arguments of false teachers.

The false teachers who had come to the region of Colosse maintained that they were bringing the people 'full riches', 'complete understanding' of spiritual truths, 'the mystery of God' and the 'hidden treasures of wisdom and knowledge'. But Paul reminded the Colossians that it is only as a person is 'in Christ' that the reality of these things are made known to him. Knowing only doctrines will not save anyone. Boasting of a higher spirituality does not bring peace with God.

Only a personal relationship with Christ who is supreme (Colossians 1:15-23) will bring a person to experience the 'full riches of complete understanding' of spiritual things. It is 'Christ in [us]' which is the 'hope of glory' (1:27). These blessings come not through accepting superior teaching from those who claim to be on a high spiritual plane, it comes through faith in the Lord Jesus Christ. This is granted to those who confess their sin (and inadequacy) and come before him with humility and repentance.

Even though Paul was prevented from being present with them (because of his imprisonment, 4:18), he was with them in his spirit. He means that when they suffer, because of the attacks of these evil teachers, then he suffers with them. Despite the separation and the pain of his chains, he was filled with joy because of the orderliness of their thinking, worship and conduct, and especially because of their firm faith in Christ (2:5).

PRACTICAL TASKS

1. Paul urges the Colossians not to be deceived by false teachers. James also uses this word. Compare the use of the word 'deceive' in Colossians 2:4 with James 1:22. Notice how the devil is described as the one who 'leads the whole world astray' in Revelation 12:9.

2. Compare Colossians 2:2-4 with Philippians 1:27-28. Notice Paul's concern that the believers should be united in love and should work together for the sake of Christ and his gospel.

SUMMARIZE IT

We have seen so far that Paul was encouraged by the firm faith and orderly conduct of the church at Colosse. He urged them to avoid 'clever people' whose mind and concern was not for a personal relationship with Christ and him crucified.

QUESTION TIME

1. Christians are exhorted to encourage one another. In which ways can we do this? (Romans 15:32; Romans 12:8; Ephesians 6:22; 1 Thessalonians 4:18; 5:11 and 5:14).

2. The truth is sometimes very painful. How can we obey Paul's injunction in Ephesians 4:15 and 'speak the truth in love'?

3. Christian love (such as Christ shed his blood to achieve) should unite God's people, not divide them. How can believers endeavour to ensure that they 'love one another' in unity? (Judges 20:11; 1 Samuel 18:1; Colossians 1:20).

THE GUIDE

CHAPTER NINE

FULNESS
IN CHRIST

LOOK IT UP

BIBLE READING

Colossians 2:6-7

WHAT THE TEXT TEACHES

Having spoken to the Colossians about the supremacy of Christ (1:15-20), their own salvation (1:21-23) and having assured them of his interest in them and concern for their spiritual welfare (1:24 - 2:5), the apostle now comes to the heart of the matter. Teachers of false doctrine were attacking all of the churches of the Lycus valley, and especially the church at Colosse. To address their needs and to help them overcome the effects of these evil teachers, Paul gives the sound and clear advice that we find in these two verses. He reminds them of their conversion to Christ and encourages them to continue in the faith rather than be led astray by false doctrines.

Their conversion

Conversion is described as their 'having received Christ'. It is not something that they achieved through their own efforts. Nowhere in the Bible does it say that a person becomes a Christian

because he or she 'decided for Christ' or because he or
she 'gave his or her heart to Jesus'. To be truly saved, a
person has to 'receive Christ Jesus as Lord'.

Here we have the three usual titles of Christ in one
statement. We do not, first of all, receive Christ as Saviour, and then, after we have gained a certain degree
of maturity, receive him as Lord. Someone has said, 'If
he is not Lord of all, he is not Lord at all.' The great
London preacher of Victorian times, C. H. Spurgeon,
tells us that the word 'Saviour' occurs only twice in
the Acts of the Apostles (Acts 5:31; 13:23), yet the title
'Lord' is mentioned ninety-two times, 'Lord Jesus' thirteen times and 'The Lord Jesus Christ' six times.[1]

The reason that Paul mentions their conversion to
Christ and their receiving of him as their Lord is so
that he can go on to tell them how they should continue to live. They were not merely to receive the 'pure
gospel message' and then stagnate. They were meant
to make progress in the Christian life. This is why Paul
urged the Colossians to 'continue to live in [Christ]'.
The vital necessity of being 'in Christ' and 'with Christ'
is emphasized in this letter. In chapter 2:6, Paul urges
the believers to 'continue to live in him' (see Colossians
1:2, 27-28; 2:7, 10-13, 20; 3:1).

Their spiritual growth

As agricultural activity was so much part of the people's
lives, Paul uses an illustration from the world of agri-
culture to indicate how a believer should continue in

the Christian life and make progress in it. Just as a plant needs to take in sustenance from the ground (or the air and rain in the case of 'tillandsias')[2], so the Christian must continually draw spiritual nourishment from Christ.

Not only do plants need to grow, babies must develop as well. Unless there is growth, the child, sadly, will become weaker and die. A baby receives its milk from its mother (or from suitable powdered baby milk); so a Christian needs to feed on Christ. He does this through the power and enabling of the Holy Spirit as he prays and studies God's Word, and enjoys fellowship with other believers.

The word 'built' that Paul uses in this verse takes us to an illustration from the world of construction. For a house to rise, it needs, first of all, to have a firm foundation, then it must have bricks or stones added to it in an appropriate way. A builder, who knows his job and does it well, builds a suitable edifice.

PRACTICAL TASKS

1. Look up Ephesians 3:17; 4:15-16 and 1 Peter 2:2 and then describe some of the ways in which Christians can be built up in Christ.

2. Read Hebrews 5:11-14 and note what the writer says about the need to progress beyond baby food.

3. Take note of the fact that these verses refer to the activity of building: Matthew 7:24-29; 1 Corinthians 3:10; Acts 20:32 and Hebrews 11:10. Write down some of the requirements for and advantages of a strong building.

Epaphras and others had taught 'the faith' to the believers at Colosse. Paul does not mean that they were taught how to put their trust in Christ. He is speaking of their adherence to the doctrines (the teachings) of the gospel. This is usually referred to as 'the faith' as opposed to 'our faith in Christ'.

The false teachers had obviously spoken to the Colossians about the need to grow up in their faith. By this they meant that they should 'go beyond' what the apostles had taught them through people like Epaphras. However, Paul counters this by telling them that they should be 'strengthened in the faith'. He means that they should be more firmly rooted in what they believe. They should be able to explain to others who Christ is, and what he has achieved on the cross to gain salvation for all those who turn away from their sins (repent) and believe in him (have faith in Christ as their only Saviour).

Their joy

Paul wanted the Colossian Christians to be 'overflowing with thankfulness'. It seems that the false teachers had been saying that if these believers followed their instructions then they would be 'overflowing' with

knowledge — that is, a sense of their own importance. Perhaps these teachers had promised them
an 'abundant life' if they followed their wrong
teaching.

Paul wanted the Colossians to understand that
their thanksgiving should be overflowing because
they were being 'built up' and strengthened 'in
the faith'. They should not be filled with thankfulness because they were more spiritually
mature than others, and not only because they
had entered into the fulness of spiritual 'wisdom
and knowledge' (2:3), but because they were up-
holding the doctrines of Christ, and all the glory
was going to him (i.e., the Lord Jesus Christ).

SUMMARIZE IT

We have seen so far that Christians are born
from above (John 3:16). They rejoice in
God's grace towards them, but they should
not remain 'infants' in the faith.

QUESTION TIME

1. In Psalm 1, the believer is described as a tree
planted by 'streams of water'. How can a Christian (tree), who has been planted by God, grow
to Christian maturity? (Psalm 1, John 4:13-14;
Revelation 22:1-2).

WORK AT IT

2. *If Paul is saying that faith in the pure gospel, as taught
   them by Epaphras, is sufficient, what does Peter mean
   when he says that believers should 'add to their faith'
   (2 Peter 1:5-7)?*

CHAPTER TEN

TRUE AND FALSE RELIGION

LOOK IT UP

BIBLE READING

Colossians 2:8-10

WHAT THE TEXT TEACHES

False philosophy

Paul emphasizes once again the need for the members of the Colossian church to be on their guard against the new teachers that had come among them and their fellow Christians in the neighbouring churches. He does this by saying, 'See to it' (which is, perhaps, more emphatic today than 'beware' which is used in the *Authorised Version*). These false teachers were out to capture them. A person, or gang, who wishes to kidnap the child of wealthy parents for a ransom payment will go about it in a subtle way. People who have evil designs will not show their true intentions as they seek to do their work. They will use exciting enticements that are aimed to gain the confidence of the child and draw him or her towards them.

In the same way, these false teachers did not act in an immoral way. In fact, they may well have lived lives that would be considered upright as far as worldly standards are concerned.

However, their aim was to 'take captive' these Colossian believers. They used philosophy which depended on human tradition and the basic principles of this world. In other words, they did not bring any strange-sounding teaching, they spoke using 'the best' type of Greek philosophy — that is, love of wisdom and Jewish traditional teaching.

Many 'religious' groups are roaming city streets today, seeking to win people to their cause. The behaviour of these people is often based upon living according to a strict moral code. They claim to have found a better way of life, a way that is free from the materialism and 'rat-race' of our modern world. Consequently, they persuade many well-intentioned people to follow them, but, like these new teachers at Colosse, they are calling them to follow a 'hollow' and 'deceptive' way of life.

It is hollow because, in the end, it holds nothing of real value. It is deceptive because it promises its followers a spiritual life of fulness that is not attainable without Christ.

PRACTICAL TASKS

1. Read 1 Corinthians 1:18-25 and note Paul's comparison between worldly wisdom and the wisdom found in Christ. List the differences.

2. Think of the kinds of words that false teachers might speak to unsuspecting Christian people and observe how these false teachers should be avoided. Read Ephesians 5:6 and

note also the warning that Peter gave concerning those who entice people away from the truth with 'empty, boastful words' in 2 Peter 2:18.

True wisdom

The test of all philosophies and religious teachings is: are they based on Christ, his salvation and his Word? From Colossians 2:9-15, Paul expounds in glorious detail what it really means to be 'in Christ'. He affirms the deity of Christ, and he says that all the fulness of this deity (i.e., God) lives in Christ in bodily form.

Here we have a clear statement that the Lord Jesus Christ was, and still is, both God and man. This is in direct contradiction to the teaching given by these visitors to the church at Colosse. Paul repeats the teaching he gave in chapter 1:19. The wonderful fulness of Christ is still found in him; it is 'living' in him in bodily form.

In verse 9, we have an even more stupendous truth. Not only is all of the fulness of the deity found in Christ, but also every believer has been 'given fulness in Christ'. This is not something that a believer attains by his own efforts; it is the gift of God. Ephesians 2:8-9 tells us that salvation comes entirely from God as his free gift to those who believe in Christ. It is not attained through our own good works. The next verse (Ephesians 2:10) says that we, as God's workmanship, have been created to do good works. In James 2:14-18 we read about the relationship between faith and good works.

The fulness of the deity is found in Christ who is far above us in every respect. So how can we be given fulness in Christ? We have already seen that this idea of 'fulness' was something that the false teachers were seeking to impart to the believers in Colosse. This is, no doubt, why Paul describes blessings in Christ in these terms.

One commentator illustrates this by saying that one day he stood beside the vast Pacific Ocean. He had a small glass jar in his hand and stooped to fill it with some of the water from the Ocean. When he held it up, it was full of sea water even though he did not have the fulness of the Pacific Ocean in his jar. He says, 'Thinking of Christ, we realize that because he is infinite, he can hold all the fulness of Deity. And whenever one of us finite creatures dips the tiny vessel of our life into him, we instantly become full of his fulness'.[1]

This same Christ, with whom we are filled, is also Head over every power and authority. This means that he reigns supremely not only over the world but also the universe. It also means that he is able and willing to protect his people from all the assaults of their enemies, both physical and spiritual.

SUMMARIZE IT

We have see so far that everything outside of Christ is empty, however good, wise or even based

on tradition it appears to be. We can only know security and power by being 'in Christ'.

QUESTION TIME

WORK AT IT

1. How would you counter the arguments of followers of Eastern religions, when they claim that they are offering the way to a more 'spiritual' life than the church is?

2. From a study of Philippians 2:5-11, what can we learn about the humanity and deity of Christ?

3. What do the following verses say about the deity of Christ: Romans 1:25; Exodus 3:13-15 and 1 Timothy 6:15?

THE GUIDE

CHAPTER ELEVEN

WHAT HAS CHRIST DONE?

BIBLE READING

Colossians 2:11-12

These verses — and the next two — speak about Christ's death, burial and resurrection. We are reminded of what we have experienced by being crucified, buried and raised again to new life in Christ.

It would seem that the false teachers were offering a deeper spiritual experience that they called 'fulness'. It may well be that this was why Paul reminded the Colossian believers that Christ had done everything that they needed for spiritual life. He speaks of what the Lord has already done for his people. This is why he writes, 'In him... you *were* also circumcised' (italics mine).

Christ's death and ours

It may be that the visitors had been speaking about the need for Christians to be circumcised. This is a Jewish ritual involving the cutting away of the foreskin. But Paul says that whether they have undergone this ceremony literally or not, it is the circumcision done by Christ (not by the hands of men) that matters. In other words, he is speaking about the circumcision of our hearts which is what Christ did for us when he died on the cross. At Calvary, he paid the price for our sins. Through faith in him we have forgiveness of sins. Therefore, we have been brought out of darkness into the light (Colossians 1:13).

Physical circumcision involves the rather violent cutting away of a piece of skin; the spiritual circumcision (done by Christ) is 'the putting off of the sinful nature'. Just as Christ died — putting off not just a small piece of his flesh, but sacrificing his whole body — so we, through his death, have put off our sinful nature.

This does not mean that we no longer sin. Sadly, that is not the case. However, it does mean that our 'sinful nature' has been crucified with Christ. Sinful desires are still with us; Satan sees to that; but we are no longer condemned by our sin (Romans 8:1). Nevertheless, we must continue to strive to break free from its pull (Colossians 3:5).

PRACTICAL TASKS

1. Carefully study Romans chapter 7 and notice what Paul says about the struggle between his spiritual nature (his new life in Christ) and his sinful nature (that with which he was born and with which he still struggled).

2. Read the verses in the letter to the Colossians that speak about our salvation as a change, symbolised in various

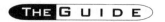

ways, for example, from darkness to light, death to life, and old to new: Colossians 1:13, 21-22; 2:13; 3:10,12.

Christ's burial and ours

The fact that the earthly body of the Lord Jesus Christ was taken down from the cross and buried was very important to the early church. If Christ had merely swooned and then revived in the cool of the borrowed tomb (as Muslims and other teach), then he could not have died to pay the penalty of our sins.

Baptism is a symbol of death — that is, being 'buried with Christ through baptism into death' (Romans 6:4). Those who baptize newly saved people by means of total immersion sometimes call the baptistery a 'watery grave'. Baptism is therefore a very powerful symbol of the believer dying to sin and being 'baptized into [Christ's] death' (Romans 6:3).

Christ's resurrection and ours

The bodily resurrection of Christ is documented in the New Testament, and many books have been written in its defence. Paul has explained the consequences of not believing in the physical resurrection of Christ. He said, 'If Christ has

WHAT THE TEXT TEACHES

not been raised then our preaching is useless and so is your faith' (1 Corinthians 15:14).

It was a mighty power that raised Christ up from death, and through faith in him, all believers have also been raised with him. In chapter 3:1 of this letter, Paul goes on to explain the implications of this fact: these Colossian believers 'have been raised with Christ'. He is not talking about the great resurrection at the last day; Paul is speaking about the present state of believers. His emphasis is not that one day the children of God will be raised up — that is true — but Paul is concerned to remind these Christian people of the present reality of new life in Christ.

PRACTICAL TASKS

1. Read Romans 6:1-10 and note that baptism is a symbol of death, resurrection and new life in Christ. There is no mention of water (either sprinkled, poured or dipped into) in this passage. It is speaking about the spiritual symbolism of baptism.

2. Study the passage in 1 Corinthians 15:3-7 and notice how the testimony of the Old Testament (Psalm 16:8-11; Isaiah 53:5-6,11) ties in with the evidence of New Testament witnesses (Acts 1:21-22).

SUMMARIZE IT

We have seen so far that the death, burial and resurrection of Christ are facts of history. But it is also something that Christians are intimately involved with. We are required to live in Christ because we have already been put to death, buried with him in baptism and raised to life again.

QUESTION TIME

WORK AT IT

1. *Why is it foolish for some to speak of the resurrection at the last day as being merely a symbolic event, or that the resurrection has already taken place when, for example, when a person first believes in Christ for salvation? (2 Timothy 2:18).*

2. *What are the spiritual benefits to the believer from the resurrection of Christ? (John 11:25; Philippians 3:10; 1 Peter 1:3).*

CHAPTER TWELVE

FROM DEATH
TO LIFE

BIBLE READING

Colossians 2:13-15

WHAT THE TEXT TEACHES

The opening words of this section paint a picture of the unconverted person as he is before Christ redeems him from his sin. Paul refers to that time as 'death'. He says that these Colossian believers were dead in their sins; their sinful nature was uncircumcised (he means that they had not yet experienced the circumcision of the heart, which only Christ can perform). The apostle explains the life of the non-Christian in greater detail in Ephesians 2:1-3.

But then God began to work and made them alive. This comes about through the life of Christ, resurrection life. When they turned away from their sin (in true God-given repentance) and turned to him (in Holy Spirit-given faith), this new life was imparted to them. This was not an act of man, or something that was performed through a religious ceremony (for example, circumcision or baptism), nor was it even achieved through their good works; it was an act of God that was accomplished through the obedience of his Son.

In reading Ephesians 2:1-10 it is possible to make two lists. The first one would show 'the state of the unsaved' and the second would describe 'the condition of a person in Christ'. In verses 1–4, we find Paul's description of those who are unsaved; they are 'dead' in transgressions and sins; they are following the ways of this world; and they are under the power and influence of the Evil One who works in those who are disobedient to God and his Word. Then there is a sharp division at verse 4. In the *Authorised Version*, this verse starts with the words 'But God' (in the *NIV*, it is merely 'But'). From this point onwards, Paul shows us the distinction between the state of the unsaved person and the condition of the one who is 'in Christ'. Because of God's mercy, those who had previously been dead in their sins had been made alive. They had been raised up with Christ, given a seat in the heavenly realms and created anew in Christ Jesus to do good works.

This same distinction is explained in Romans 5:19. Paul describes the unsaved person as being disobedient to God and his law. This unsaved person originally had a sinful nature; he was like Adam, disobedient to God's command (Genesis 3:1-7). Then the contrast comes. This 'disobedient' (i.e., sinful) person has been made righteous. And this has come about solely through Christ's obedience to his Father's will.

The blessings of our salvation

Once again Paul mentions the forgiveness of sins. Sin is an impenetrable barrier that keeps us from God. Even all of the sacrifices offered by priests in Old Testament times could not take away sin. Today the words and actions of a multitude of priests, religious leaders, gurus and the latest philosophers cannot take away sin either. However, through the death of God's spotless 'Lamb' (the Lord Jesus Christ), sin has been taken away. He did not merely overlook our sin: '[He] who had no sin [became] sin for us' (2 Corinthians 5:21). Through his death on the cross, Christ has borne the punishment that was due to us and has forgiven each and every one of our sins.

The apostle then goes on in greater detail to explain how this has happened. The list of our sins is long and detailed. It has been written down so that it can be used as evidence against us at the Day of Judgement. However, through the cross, God has cancelled that debt which was against us, and which stood against us. The regulations of the Law of God demanded that we obey them, but, through our frailty and natural inclination to sinful thinking and actions, we have broken them time without number and in countless ways. Our thoughts, our words and our actions have often been motivated by our old sinful nature, which still lurks within us.

When Christ was executed, a notice was written and nailed over his cross (John 19:19). This was displayed for all to see. Pilate intended this to be an accusation against Christ. Yet Christ was, and remained, sinless. Nevertheless, death on a tree brought a curse upon the crucified (Deuteronomy 21:23; Galatians 3:13). 'The curse and its condemnation of broken law belonged to the Colossians before their conversion. It has now been set aside, not in the sense of being overlooked and ignored, but because in Christ it has already been exhausted — and the Colossians are now in Christ, able to share in all the benefits of his substitutionary and atoning death'.[1]

Not only did Christ achieve our salvation when he died upon the cross for us, but God also defeated Satan and all the hosts of evil. On the cross, Christ overcame the dreadful powers of sin, Satan and this world. Although Satan is a defeated foe, he is still active in this world. However, Christ made a public spectacle of him and all that is evil, 'triumphing over them by the cross' (v. 15).

Paul is probably referring to the grand reception given to Generals, who returned victorious from the battlefield to the loud acclaim of the people. During this procession, sweet spices were burned in the streets and the petals were strewn on the road. Also in the procession were those who had been taken captive. The aroma of the spices and the scent of the flowers (which was released as the soldiers crushed them under their feet) was a sweet aroma to the victorious men. However,

WORK AT IT

it was a smell that reminded the captives of their imminent death.

1. Compare Deuteronomy 21:23 with its quotations in Galatians 3:13 and Acts 5:30. Galatians 3:14 records the blessings received through Christ. Make a note of the blessings that Christ has obtained for his people through the curse of the cross.

2. Read about 'the triumphal procession in Christ' in 2 Corinthians 2:14-16. Then explain how we can be an aroma 'of Christ', both to those who are being saved and to those who are perishing.

SUMMARIZE IT

We have seen so far that before conversion we are dead in sin. But when we were 'made alive', we experienced forgiveness of all our sins and the cancellation of the debt against us.

QUESTION TIME

1. How would you explain the danger of remaining in sin to an unsaved person? (Isaiah 1:2-6; Ephesians 2:12; 1 Thessalonians 4:13).

2. *What difference does the cross make to your spiritual life, and how do you demonstrate its blessings to the unsaved as you go about your daily work?*

CHAPTER THIRTEEN

BEWARE OF THOSE WHO SAY, 'BEWARE!'

LOOK IT UP

BIBLE READING

Colossians 2:13-15

WHAT THE TEXT TEACHES

Food and special days

Having just reminded the Colossians of their new life in Christ, Paul then proceeds to urge them to let nothing, or no one, take that assurance from them. He gives the warning, 'Do not let anyone' at the beginning of verse 16 and again at the start of verse 18.

It would seem that the false teachers who had come to the region stipulated that their followers should observe certain rituals before they could experience the 'fulness of blessing' in Christ. The two matters that Paul refers to in verse 16 (regulations concerning 'diet' and certain 'days') were both commanded to be observed in Old Testament times. We can see some of the reasoning behind these commands. When the Israelites were walking through the desert, without the aid of refrigerators, it was hygienic to drain the blood from a slaughtered animal before cooking and eating it. Also the regulations concerning food outlined in Leviticus chapter 11 were humane because they were designed to ensure, among other things, that the slaughtered animal suffered as little as possible. Clearly the 'visitors' were teaching the Colossians (many of whom were Gentiles) that they were in great error if they disobeyed the food regulations of the Old Testament.

With regard to holy days, the false teachers were advocating the same obedience to the Old Testament system. Leviticus chapter 25 refers to special feast days, and other parts of the Old Testament mention 'new moon' celebrations and Sabbaths (1 Chronicles 23:31 and Isaiah 1:13). We see, then, that 'the Sabbaths' was a term used to describe annual, monthly and weekly celebrations.

In verse 17 of Colossians chapter 2, Paul shatters the words of the false teachers. This verse is a like a bright light shining upon them (and us). Paul states very clearly that food laws and the observing of special religious days were merely a shadow of the things that were to come.

The apostle was not saying that they should cast aside all previous requirements and eat whatever they fancied, nor was he saying that they should ignore special events in their calendars, he was emphasizing that they were no longer bound by legalism. Christ had fulfilled the law, and the Old Testament regulations found their fulfilment in him. Because Christ had come as the fulfilment of the symbols, why should the Colossians observe the shadow when they had the blessings of the reality? It is like watching, over and over again, a film of a young cherry tree, which was taken ten years previously, and admiring the buds beginning to swell, containing within them the promise of a lovely bloom, when instead of watching the film, the door of the house could be opened and the sight of the mature cherry tree in full bloom could be enjoyed right now.

We can find further illustrations of the New Testament teaching on food laws. In Mark 7:18-20 and Matthew 15:1-20, we have Jesus' teaching on the things that go into and come out of a person. Acts 10:13-16 tells us what Peter learned on his way to see the Gentile, Cornelius. Furthermore, Paul said, 'Food does not bring us nearer to God; we are no worse if we do not eat, and no better if we do' (1 Corinthians 8:8). However, the apostle went on to warn the Corinthian Christians to be careful that they did not exercise their freedom in such a way that it became a stumbling block to the weak. In other words, although it was perfectly acceptable for them to eat food that had previously been offered to idols, they should not do so in a thoughtless way that could lead someone astray who was not yet prepared to turn aside from a legalistic upbringing.

With regard to the command to 'remember the Sabbath day by keeping it holy' (Exodus 20:8), we need to realize that this command has not been cancelled; its purpose has been more fully explained by the Lord himself.

In the days of the early church many slaves became Christians. Did their pagan masters give them a day off each week so that they could keep the Sabbath day holy? Certainly not, they had to meet for worship with their fellow-believers on those occasions when they had some time off, but they were not excommunicated from the church because they obeyed their masters and worked on the Sabbath day. The reason for this was because Jesus had explained that 'the Sabbath was made for man' (i.e., for his benefit). In other words, the Sabbath was no longer to be kept in a legalistic way; it had been given by the Lord to bring rest and blessing to those who obeyed it.

However, the emphasis in the New Testament is not on the Sabbath (seventh) day, but on the first day of the week. Groups like the Seventh Day Adventists believe that the Christian church had no right to change the 'day of rest' from the seventh to the first day (the Greek word for Saturday is *Sabbato*). To find out what the early church did about the command to keep the Sabbath day holy, we need to read the New Testament and notice on which days they met for corporate worship.

Just after the day of Pentecost we read that '*every* day [the believers] continued to meet together in the temple courts. They broke bread in their homes and ate together with glad and sincere hearts, praising God' (Acts 2:46-47, italics mine). But in the Corinthian church we find that Paul commanded the believers to set aside a sum of money 'on *the first day of every week*' (1 Corinthians 16:2, italics mine) and Luke tells us that at Troas the believers came together to break bread 'on *the first day of the week*' (Acts 20:7, italics mine). Even though they stayed in that place for seven days, we are not told that they broke bread every day. It would seem, then, that the early church moved the observance of the Sabbath day to the following day: the first day of the week. This is further emphasized when we turn to the last book in the Bible. When John was an old man imprisoned on the island of Patmos, he heard behind him a loud voice, and he specifically tells us the day on which this occurred. He says that he heard that voice on '*the Lord's Day*' (Revelation 1:10, italics mine). Surely by 'the Lord's Day' he meant the day on which Jesus Christ rose from the dead. John's account in his Gospel tells us which day that was. He rose on 'the first day of the week' (John 20:1).

When I visited the land of Israel, I discovered that the Jewish and Palestinian Christian churches hold their services on Saturdays because this is the day which everyone in Israel has off; it is the Jewish Sabbath. When God's people reach heaven they will obtain their eternal rest. They will not meet for worship on the seventh or the first day of the week; their worship of the Lord will last for all eternity. In the meantime the principle to be obeyed is that one day in seven (either Saturday or Sunday) should be taken as rest from all normal work.

False humility

Genuine humility is a Christian virtue that should be sought after; we are urged to humble ourselves under God's mighty hand (1 Peter 5:6). The person who claims to be very 'religious' but in fact is full of 'false humility' is easily recognized by the true Christian as a fraud. Such teachers urge people to listen to tales of what they have seen in visions and 'spiritual daydreams'. They may speak with a sickening pretence of humility about their inadequacy to approach God. Paul condemns such people. He says, 'Beware of these who want to judge you because of your simple allegiance to Christ and his teaching. They want to turn you away from the pure gospel of salvation, but if you follow them you will be disqualified for "the prize". These people, who disqualify you because you have not kept the rules for Christian living, claim to have the right to be umpires, but, in fact, they have cut themselves off from the Head of the church.' Paul goes on to explain that these false teachers are not growing because they have lost connection with the Head. In other words, they are demonstrating that they have a defective view of Christ and his teaching.

WORK AT IT

1. Look up the following references and make a list of the dangers of 'pride': Proverbs 16:18; Obadiah 3; 1 Corinthians 4:18; 5:2; 13:4.

2. Look up the following and make a list of the blessings of true humility: Proverbs 16:19; Isaiah 57:15; Micah 6:8; James 4:6; 1 Peter 5:6.

3. Read the following scriptures: Ephesians 1:22; 4:6; 1 Corinthains 12:27-31 and describe the church of God as a body, noting the importance of the Head.

False wisdom

In the closing verses of chapter 2, we have more details of the teaching and behaviour of the false teachers who were plaguing the church at Colosse.

Once again Paul speaks firmly to the Colossian believers in order to bring them to their senses. It is as though he was crying out to them, 'Why do you imagine that you are gaining spiritual maturity by merely observing rules about physical actions? You are dead to all of this. You died with Christ, so why are you so concerned to obey earthly rules?'

Food, special days and harsh treatment of our bodies will never bring us nearer to God; only holy living in obedience to Christ will bring us blessing. It is not only the Muslim or Hindu fakir who draws many to himself by his ascetic lifestyle. The Christian groups who demand complete obedience to their leaders and who impose strict rules of discipline, are in danger of giving an appearance of wisdom, whereas without Christian humility, they are leading many astray.

SUMMARIZE IT

We have seen so far that we should not allow anyone to judge us concerning our observance of man-made or Old Testament regulations which have been fulfilled in Christ. We should not live our lives by worldly principles, but by Christ's teaching.

QUESTION TIME

1. *In what ways were the laws of the Old Testament a shadow of the things that were to come? (Hebrews 8:5; 10:1-14).*

2. *How would you deal with a person who claims to have received special revelation from God, and who goes into great detail about what he has seen? Notice what*

little detail Paul gives about the 'man caught up to the third heaven' (2 Corinthians 12:1-4).

3. What effect on a congregation might a person have who knows his Bible thoroughly, has studied theology and is equipped with a fine intelligence, but has no personal contact with Christ, the living Head?

4. In Christ, the Colossians had died to the basic principles of this world, yet they still submitted to its rules. In what ways do Christian people today live by the rules of worldliness? (1 John 2:15-17; Romans 12:2; 1 Corinthians 1:20; 2 Corinthians 10:2; Ephesians 4:17-24; Psalm 119:36; James 3:13-16).

CHAPTER FOURTEEN

THE CHRISTIAN MINDSET

LOOK IT UP

BIBLE READING

Colossians 3:1-4

WHAT THE TEXT TEACHES

A heart set on things above

Having warned the Colossians of dangers (2:8,16,18), Paul now proceeds to urge them to live the Christian life without worldly rules or worldly wisdom. Not only have they died with Christ (2:20), but they have also been raised to life with Christ. He tells the Romans, 'If we have been united with him … in his death, we will certainly also be united with him in his resurrection' (Romans 6:5). In Christ, his blood-bought people have new (resurrection) life.

They no longer take notice of those who demand that they follow earthly rules to gain 'fulness in Christ'; they look above where Christ is now seated at the right hand of God. However, the Christian's desire to look above is not to obtain material blessings (as depicted in the Medieval Church painters); he looks above for spiritual realities. It is above in heaven where the believer's true treasure lies (Matthew 6:19-24).

The Colossians must make it their earnest endeavour to set their hearts on things above. They should not use their time striving to obey earthly rules, nor observing regulations that only have the appearance of wisdom (2:20-23), their great desire should be to look to heaven and Christ who is 'the hope of glory' (1:27). They should set their hearts on these things, not the things of the flesh.

PRACTICAL TASKS

1. Psalm 110:1 says, 'The LORD says to my Lord: "Sit at my right hand until I make your enemies a footstool for your feet."' This verse is quoted in the New Testament more often than any other. Look up the following references and make notes on how this quotation is used: Matthew 22:44; 26:64; Mark 12:36; 14:62; 16:19; Luke 20:42-43; 22:69; 1 Corinthians 15:25; Acts 2:34-35; Ephesians 1:20; Colossians 3:1; Hebrews 1:3,13, 8:1; 10:13 and 1 Peter 3:22.

2. Jesus said, 'Where you treasure is, there your heart will be also' (Matthew 6:21). Study this section of 'The Sermon on the Mount' (Matthew 6:19-24) and compare it to the two stories of the rich men in Luke 12:13-21 and Luke 18:18-30.

A mind set on things above[1]

What we think in our minds so often guides our subsequent actions. If we are to prevent our hearts from wandering from the person we love, then we should

WHAT THE TEXT TEACHES

not allow our thoughts to dwell upon the attractive features of another. If we are to refrain from reading unedifying material, then we should stop going to the shop where such literature is displayed. At the very least, we should stay away from the shelves where these books are placed. Paul has already told the Colossians to set their hearts on things above; now he urges them to do the same thing with their minds. We have already seen that Paul regularly refers to our hearts and our minds.

Not only are we to direct our emotions to 'things above', we are also to set our minds in that direction. Because we live on this earth and spend many hours earning our living in our secular occupations, we should not allow the standards of this world to dominate our spiritual lives. This does not mean that we should cut ourselves off from the world. If we did so, we would not be able to witness to the Lord Jesus Christ and his great salvation, nor would we be an influence for good in the communities where we live. The monk or nun who shuts him or herself away from the world cannot escape the corruption of his or her own heart.

Every believer has died with Christ and therefore is hidden with Christ in God. This means that believers have double security. The people of the world look at the church and see the outward signs of the devil's influence. They so often see selfishness, pride and greed. However, the beauty and glory of Christ lie hidden inside the believer and in the godly church. The false teachers were promising fulness of knowledge by following their teaching, but Christ offers to those who follow the doctrines of the apostles, the security of being hidden in the One, in whom 'all the treasures of wisdom and knowledge' are found (2:3). In Galatians 2:20 the apostle explained it like this: 'I have been crucified with Christ and I no longer live, but Christ lives in me. The life I live in the body, I live by faith in the Son of God, who loved me and gave himself for me.'

The believer, who has been raised with Christ, has a new life that can be summed up in one word: 'Christ'. The Lord Jesus Christ is everything to him. He cannot bear to hear others take his Lord's name in vain by using it as a swear word. He cannot lie down to sleep without first calling on the name of the Lord and giving him praise and thanksgiving for the day which has gone past. He cannot wake up in the morning without worshipping him, and seeking his help and strength for the day that lies ahead.

The worldly person cannot understand this attitude because the only thing he is aware of is this corrupt world and its evil ways. However, the saved person has a new life, one that is 'hidden with Christ in God' (v. 3). Because of this, he is secure and safe from all the harm that the world, or the devil, can throw at him.

The believer is not only safe with Christ, but he also knows that one day Christ will return to this earth; he will 'appear'. It is for this great event that he eagerly waits. This is why the believer has his mind prepared for action. He is self-controlled, and he has 'set [his] hope fully on the grace to be given [him] when Jesus Christ is revealed' (1 Peter 1:13; 1 Corinthians 1:7). Then the life of the Christian, which the world has despised, 'will also be revealed as something which will abide for ever'.[2] John tells us that 'when [Christ] appears, we shall be like him, for we shall see him as he is' (1 John 3:2).

SUMMARIZE IT

We have seen so far that the heart and the mind of the believer must be directed upwards where Christ is seated at God's right hand. We have died to worldly demands, and are now hidden with Christ in God, with whom we will one day appear in glory.

QUESTION TIME

DISCUSS IT

1. How can we set our hearts and minds on 'things above' when we live in a selfish and demanding world? (1 Peter 1:13; Philippians 2:1-11).

2. *How should we be living now, in view of Christ's return to this earth in the future? (2 Peter 3:11-12; 2 Corinthians 6:14-18; 1 Thessalonians 4:1; Hebrews 9:14).*

THE GUIDE

CHAPTER FIFTEEN

PUT TO DEATH OLD DESIRES

LOOK IT UP

⟨BIBLE READING⟩

Colossians 3:5-11

WHAT THE TEXT TEACHES

The word 'therefore' in verse 5 takes us back to what Paul was saying in verses 1–4 of this chapter. Because Christians are now 'hidden with Christ in God', they must put to death everything that is alien to Christ. They have died to sin (2:20); they have been buried with Christ (symbolized in Christian baptism, 2:12); they have been raised with Christ (3:1); and have ascended with him — in the sense of 'looking above', where he is seated at God's right hand (3:4). Because of all this, Christians must now live in accordance with their standing in Christ.

Christian doctrine is not something that should be kept hidden away in our hearts, even though the reality of it is hidden from the unsaved. It should be demonstrated in the street and in our homes — that is, in our public and private lives. Following his normal method of outlining Christian teaching, the apostle Paul then goes on to apply it to his readers. He was so determined to ensure that the believers at Colosse were living 'in Christ' that he used very strong language to stress its importance. This is why he says, 'Put to death … whatever belongs to your earthly nature.' The earthly nature seeks to prevent progress in the Christian life that is why it is to be 'put to death'. This is a painful and difficult process, but the Christian who wants to live for Christ's glory must do it without timidity.

Our earthly nature

Paul lists five evils — as an illustration of many — that come from our earthly nature. These were things that were abhorred by the religious people of Jesus' time. These are sinful desires that are conceived in the mind. The person who commits immoral acts has first of all thought about them and then planned them.

Immorality covers all kinds of sinful sensuality. The word *pornographic* is derived from the same Greek word as the term sexual immorality. This gives rise in the worldly person (and, sadly, in the Christian also) to all kinds of evil desires and greed that seek to satisfy our 'lower' nature.

In the Greek world of Paul's day, such behaviour was common. Even today the sign for the brothel can be seen clearly engraved in the pathway near the library in ancient Ephesus. These ladies not only satisfied the lusts of the Ephesian men, their earnings also swelled the coffers of the city's treasury. In Corinth, these things were done in the name of religion. It is

WHAT THE TEXT TEACHES

said that the temple of Apollo housed huge numbers of 'temple' prostitutes.

No one can say that this letter to the Colossians is 'out of date', because all around us in our world today there are many alluring images used in advertisements, in newspapers, magazines and on television. These are designed to entice people to lust for sexual gratification. In Paul's day, the people were making an idol of sex; it is the same today. Such things amount to greed: the desire to satisfy the sinful nature, regardless of the cost or the consequences.

It is because of such sins that the wrath of God threatens to come down on this world. Sensual lust makes a mockery of that which God made beautiful, for the exclusive enjoyment of a husband and wife.

PRACTICAL TASKS

1. Notice the division between the parts of Paul's letters which are mainly doctrinal and the practical sections; the teaching is stated first and the application of those truths follows on from the doctrines. Notice a clear division that comes at Ephesians 4:1 and Romans 12:1.

2. In times past, and still in some countries today, thieves have their hands cut off. This may prevent them stealing things with their hands, but they can still use their teeth, or employ others to do their evil

work. Only the mortification of our earthly nature will cure us of sinful desires. Study Mark 7:14-23 and take note of where the Lord says evil springs from.

Our earthly words ᵛˢ 8 - 11

Together with the five sensual lusts in verse 5, Paul lists five aspects of human behaviour that spring from an uncontrolled mind. These are sins that manifest themselves in words, aggressive words. These are the words that flow from a person who has a quick temper, who speaks before carefully considering the effects of his or her words. Malice is a mind that plans evil against others, while slander has the intention of defaming someone's character. Unchecked, these things will lead to filthy language: foul, obscene and abusive speech.

These were the sorts of things the Colossians indulged in before they became Christians. But now they have new life in Christ and they must embark upon a deliberate course of action which has as its objective the eradicating of these things from their thoughts and actions. They knew exactly what Paul meant because they used to live like this. Therefore, he requires that they put off such sinful behaviour because they have put on the new self.

This new self is being renewed in knowledge in the image of its Creator. How can people from different backgrounds and varying intellectual ability live in genuine unity? They experience renewal only through Christ. When they are saved, they are brought out of darkness and into the light (1:13). This means that they have an entirely different relationship with God, and also with one another. It is not only the Jews who experience a 'national' unity; Gentiles are also brought into the kingdom (1:27). Circumcision no longer causes a barrier between God's people. The 'uncouth Scythian from northern Greece' relates to 'the sophisticated freeman of Athens'.[1]

True unity is found among God's people when their former hatreds and immoral ways are put off and the new nature put on. Differences of race, upbringing and education no longer divide God's people; Christ is all, and in all. It is Christ and his wishes for his people that matter above all things.

In 1 Corinthians 6:9-10 we read a list of evil deeds. This is how some of the Corinthians, and also, no doubt, some of the Colossians, had been living. But what a change came over them when they were wrought upon by the Holy Spirit and came to believe in the Lord Jesus as their Saviour. Paul tells them, 'But you were washed, you were sanctified, you were justified in the name of the Lord Jesus Christ and by the Spirit of our God (1 Corinthians 6:11).

The Scriptures also tell us about the evil brought about by anger. In Ephesians 4:26-27, Paul quotes from Psalm 4:4 where he writes, 'In your anger do not sin.' Then, in Ephesians, he adds to this, 'Do not let the sun go down while you are still angry, and do not give the devil a foothold'. In Matthew, Jesus states it even more directly, 'I tell you that anyone who is angry with his brother will be subject to judgement. Again, anyone who says to his brother, "Raca," is answerable to the Sanhedrin. But anyone who says, "You fool!" will be in danger of the fire of hell' (Matthew 5:22).

QUESTION TIME

1. *2 Corinthians 4:4 states that 'the god of this age has blinded the minds of unbelievers, so that they cannot see the light of the gospel of the glory of Christ'. In what ways has Satan blinded the minds of people today, and how are the effects of his actions evident? (2 Corinthians 3:14-16; 4:1-6; Hebrews 3:19; John 3:36; Romans 11:25).*

2. *How can a Christian put off' the things that belong to his sinful nature? (Psalm 1:1-3; 119:9-11; Proverbs 4:20-27; James 3:1-6).*

CHAPTER SIXTEEN

CLOTHES TO PUT ON

BIBLE READING

Colossians 3:12-17

WHAT THE TEXT TEACHES

Paul tells the Colossians that they are 'God's chosen people'. This was a term that was used for Israel. God set his affection upon Israel and chose them for no other reason than this: he loved them (Deuteronomy 7:7-8). In Colossians 3:12, Paul speaks of those characteristics of Israel — 'chosen', 'holy' and 'beloved' — and applies them to the Colossians, and to all of those who have been redeemed by the precious blood of Christ.

The 'clothes' Christians must own

Again, five qualities are listed that should belong to Christians. The word 'compassion' signifies tenderness of heart. In the world of Paul's day, generally speaking, the maimed, sickly and aged were considered to be a nuisance and were therefore overlooked. Often the mentally ill were treated inhumanly.[1] But the members of the new Israel (the church) must treat all people with compassion. William Barclay tells us that probably 'everything that has been done for the aged, the sick, the weak in body and in the mind, the animal, the child, the woman has been done under the inspiration of Christianity'.[2]

Kindness is something that does not happen naturally because we all have a bias towards selfishness (see 'greed' in 3:5). Kindness is listed in Galatians 5:22 as one of the fruits of the Spirit. God's kindness leads us to repentance (Romans 2:4).

Humility is something that is continually stressed in the New Testament. This was a foreign concept to the Greeks, who saw humility as a weakness. However, this same word is used to describe Christ's humbling of himself by becoming obedient to death (Philippians 2:8). Jesus invited his followers to learn from him because he was lowly in heart (Matthew 11:29).

Gentleness is called 'meekness' in the *Authorised Version* of the Bible. Like humility, gentleness is not a weakness. Moses is described as being 'very meek' (Numbers 12:3, AV). Yet, he was a great leader who could act decisively.

Finally, patience is another fruit of the Spirit (Galatians 5:22). This is not a passive attitude towards life, it is a positive spirit of endurance, despite the problems that may arise. God's people are required to be patient with everyone (1 Thessalonians 5:14).

The 'clothes' a Christian must wear

It is not sufficient to own these qualities; we have to display them for the benefit of other people. The person who is 'in Christ' does not think selfishly. He bears with the faults and failings of his fellow Christians and is ready to forgive his brothers and sisters when they irritate him.

He remembers that when he trusted Christ as his Saviour, his sins were removed from him 'as far as the east is from the west' (Psalms 103:12). Jesus taught his disciples to pray, 'Forgive us our sins, for we also forgive everyone who sins against us' (Luke 11:4). Therefore, the believer must forgive 'whatever grievances' (Colossians 3:13) he may have against others within the fellowship.

In this section, Paul is, once again, returning to his great theme of the unity of the church. This unity is not to come from the edicts of a bishop or elder. It comes about solely through love. 'Christ loved the church and gave himself up for her to make her holy' (Ephesians 5:25-26). Christian people are required to 'put on' the greatest of all virtues: love. It is love that binds all of these other graces together in perfect unity.

PRACTICAL TASKS

1. Look up the following scripture references and see how the blessings of Israel have been granted to the

church of Jesus Christ: Exodus 19:5-6; Deuteronomy 7:6-8; Romans 8:33; Philippians 3:3; 1 Peter 2:9; Revelation 1:6.

2. Look up other passages where Paul speaks about the Christian's clothing: Philippians 2:3; 2 Corinthians 6:6; Galatians 5:22-23 and make notes on these qualities.

3. In Paul's first letter to the Corinthian church, he had to deal with many problems, especially in chapters 11, 12 and 14. Read very carefully his instructions to this troubled church in chapter 13. Then read Ephesians 4:2-3 and verse 32 and note how love and forgiveness bring about unity in the church.

The clothing of peace

In Colossians 1:20, Paul had reminded the Colossians that through the blood shed on the cross, Christ had made peace. Therefore, just as Christ's peace reconciles 'all things to himself', so the believers at Colosse should not live with any hatred or contempt for one another because this would militate against peace in the congregation. 'When Christ rules in the heart, his peace will rule in the fellowship.'³ When peace is in evidence in a church, then there will be much thankfulness.

The Colossians must take their instructions, not from false teachers who promise them much, but from 'the word of Christ'. We, living in the twenty-first century, have that word written down for us. In Paul's day, it was faithfully relayed from the apostles through people like Epaphras (1:7).

Visits from the early church leaders to churches like the one at Colosse were few and far between. Indeed, it seems that Paul never visited that church (Colossians 2:1). Who, then, was to do the teaching? It was ordinary believers at Colosse who were to 'teach and admonish one another' (v. 16). How would they know what to teach? They would only find out by letting 'the word of Christ dwell in [them] richly' (v. 16). They would not find wisdom from these visiting false teachers; they would discover it in the word of Christ. Those who read and meditate deeply on the Scriptures will be richly blessed.

Those who love the word of Christ and who teach its principles will be thankful, wise and joyful. Even if they do not have naturally melodious voices, they will wish to sing praises to God. The 'psalms, hymns and spiritual songs' they sing will not reflect their own triumphs and aspirations; they will be filled with heartfelt thanksgiving and praise to God who has done so much for them.

Everything they do and say will be done in the name of the Lord Jesus, and will reflect the thankfulness that they have for God the Father through Christ. Before his crucifixion, Jesus told his disciples of the peace he was giving them. All those who put their trust in Christ alone for their salvation will receive this wonderful blessing of peace (John 14:27; Numbers 6:24-26; Psalm

85:8; Malachi 2:5-6; Luke 2:14; 24:36; John 16:33; Philippians 4:7).

SUMMARIZE IT

We have seen so far that the church is a place where believers should be united in love and peace. They demonstrate their unity with praise and thanksgiving to God, and all of their actions and words spring from their love for Christ.

QUESTION TIME

1. *If we are 'God's chosen people', how should we behave towards one another? (Luke 6:36-38; John 13:14,34; Ephesians 5:1-2).*

2. *When two or more people in the same church refuse to speak to each other what action should the leaders take in an attempt to bring about reconciliation? (Galatians 6:1; 2 Corinthians 2:5-8; Philippians 4:2; 2:2; James 4:1-2.)*

CHAPTER SEVENTEEN

A CHRISTIAN'S FAMILY LIFE

LOOK IT UP

BIBLE READING

Colossians 3:18-21

WHAT THE TEXT TEACHES

At the end of chapter 3:17, Paul was urging the Colossians to 'do all in the name of the Lord Jesus'. He was not thinking solely about 're-ligious' and 'church' affairs when he said that thanks should be given to God the Father, he was also applying this principle to the home and the working life of every true Christian.

Wives and Husbands

These two verses (3:18-19), which are so simple and straightforward to us, must have had a revo-lutionary cry to the members of the Colossian church two thousand years ago. This was new, Christ-honouring teaching that Paul was giving to the believers. However, the apostle did not give this teaching to the Colossians alone; as with so much in this letter, he uses similar words to the church at Ephesus (Ephesians 5:22 - 6:9). This is not surprising, as both of these letters, together with the one to the Philippians, were written at about the same time, c. A. D. 60.

In Paul's day, women had few rights. 'Under Jewish law a woman was a thing; she was the possession of her husband, just as much as his house or his flocks or his material goods were. She had no legal rights whatever. For instance, under Jewish law (which is was not based on God's Word), a husband could divorce his wife for any cause, while a wife had no rights whatever in the initiation of divorce. In Greek society a respectable woman lived a life of entire seclusion. She never appeared on the streets alone, not even to go marketing. She lived in the women's apartments and did not join her menfolk even for meals. From her there was demanded a complete servitude and chastity; but her husband could go out as much as he chose, and could enter into as many relationships outside marriage as he liked and incur no stigma. Both under Jewish and under Greek laws and custom, all the privileges belonged to the husband, and all the duties to the wife.'[1]

With these simple words to the Colossian believers, Paul dashed such thinking to the ground. The gospel brought new respectability and responsibility to husbands and wives, children and fathers, and also to slaves and masters. No longer was the wife commanded to do what her husband decided was fitting; she was to submit to her husband only in those things which were fitting to *the Lord*. The 'right' that a husband had over his wife was to love her and care for her. He was to do this in a sacrificial way and follow the example of the

Lord who 'loved the church and gave himself up for her' (Ephesians 5:25).

In submitting to her husband, a wife is not taking a subservient, menial position. She has left her father and mother and has been united to her husband and has 'become one flesh' with him (Genesis 2:24). She is his helper and his support. She is not inferior to her husband because they are 'heirs together of the grace of life' (1 Peter 3:7, AV), but she is to submit to him as Sarah obeyed Abraham (1 Peter 3:6). She is to do this when he leads her in ways that are godly and biblical.

PRACTICAL TASKS

WORK AT IT

1. The fact that the Christian woman is to be her husband's helper in no way suggests that she is inferior to him.[2] Look up the following scripture references and notice that God (the Father) is described as our helper: Exodus 18:4; Deuteronomy 33:27-29; Psalm 46:1; 118:7.

2. Christ is not ashamed to know that God the Father, with whom he is equal, is his head. Study the following scriptures to see this truth: 1 Corinthians 11:3; 15:28.

3. Work carefully through Ephesians 5:22-6:9 and note the similarities to and the differences from Colossians 3:18-4:1.

Children and Fathers

Again, as with wives and husbands, Paul mentions the submissive one first. This time children are required to obey their parents. A home without discipline is an unhappy one. Those parents who indulge their children by giving them whatever they want or who treat their children unkindly, as though they should be 'seen and not heard', are not only behaving in ways that are unscriptural, they are also making difficulties for themselves in the future. It is very likely that these children will grow up selfish and uncaring about the feelings of others; and they may end up in trouble.

The Bible makes it very clear that parents who love their children will bring them up with just and honest discipline. The father who 'spares the rod' — either because he is frightened of upsetting his child, or because he is too busy with other things — is demonstrating that he does not love his son (Proverbs 13:24). However, while Paul urges children to be obedient to their parents, he does not give the child's father licence to treat his son cruelly or insensitively, or, indeed, in any way that will embitter or exasperate him.

While parents are addressed in verse 20, it is the father alone to whom verse 21 is directed. When children are very small, they are usually easy to amuse. A father may well look forward to coming home from a hard days work then and getting down on the floor to play with them. However, it may be a different story when the children are teenagers and their father arrives

home tired and irritable, only to discover that the children have been misbehaving. In effect, Paul says, 'Be careful how you speak and act in such circumstances. You are tired and you do not yet know all the facts. Do not say or do anything that might discourage your children. Certainly discipline them, but do so in a way that shows that you love them. Your discipline is not to make you feel better. It should be calculated to bring them back into a loving relationship with you and the rest of the family.'

SUMMARIZE IT

We have seen so far the importance of right and loving relationships between wives and husbands, and children and parents, particularly fathers.

QUESTION TIME

1. Under what conditions might it be in order for a father to smack his child? (Hebrews 12:4-12, especially verse 11; Proverbs 3:11; 13:24; 23:13; Jeremiah. 30:11; Revelation 3:19).

2. How can 'painful' discipline be carried out in a loving and biblical way? (See Hebrews 12:4-13; Psalm 94:12; 119:67; Lamentations 3:33).

WORK AT IT

3. *In the Bible, there is a reference to the fact that David had never disciplined his son, Adonijah (1 Kings 1:6). It seems likely that David had not disciplined Absolom either. What can happen when a child has not been trained in the way he should go? (1 Samuel 13 – 20 and Proverbs 22:6).*

CHAPTER EIGHTEEN

A CHRISTIAN'S
WORKING LIFE

BIBLE READING

Colossians 3:22 - 4:1

Just as children are to obey their parents in everything (3:20), so are slaves to obey their earthly masters in everything.

Slavery was common all over the Roman Empire. It is said that there were 60,000,000 slaves in the days in which this letter was written, and they numbered about half of the total population of the Empire. This means that slaves did almost all the work that was carried out. Even doctors and teachers were slaves. However, slaves had no rights of their own and they were often treated with extreme cruelty. Because they were merely 'property', when they were no longer fit to work hard, they were sometimes pushed aside and left to starve like a worn out farm implement which was of no further use to its owner.

The teaching of the New Testament condemns such behaviour. Indeed, its emphasis is on freedom. So, why did Paul not urge the slaves to revolt against these appalling conditions? It may well have been that his concern was for individual Christians, including slaves. He did not have on his agenda to incite the masses and cause a revolutionary uprising; he wanted to see men, women and children brought to a personal faith in Christ so that they would live lives which were pleasing to God and beneficial to those around them.

The duties of slaves

At first glance, the apostle seems to be teaching that slaves should accept their circumstances and do their best, despite poor conditions. But Paul was teaching something much more positive. He said, 'Slaves *obey* your masters in *everything*' (italics mine). They were to do the unpleasant jobs with the same enthusiasm they had for those that were enjoyable. They were to work hard, not only when their masters were looking at them. They were to have a sincere (a true and honest) desire to achieve good results, regardless of the circumstances. They were to understand that God is honoured when his people serve others with loyalty.

This was a completely new way of thinking. Just as the cruel taskmasters had beaten the Israelites with whips to make them work faster (Exodus 5:14), so the slaves of Paul's day worked well on those occasions when they were being observed. They did this not only to avoid punishment, but also in the hope of winning their master's favour.

The slave had no rights and he also had no hope of inheriting anything from anyone. Yet Paul says, 'Whatever you do, work at it with all your heart, as working

for the Lord.' Although his master gave the orders, the Christian slave was not so much working for his owner, he was working for the Lord. And it is the Lord himself who will reward him, with an inheritance. At the last day, everyone will be judged for what he has done wrong. Both masters and slaves will be repaid for what they have done amiss; there is no favouritism with God.

PRACTICAL TASKS

1. In Christ, all people are equal in status. Study the following scriptures which emphasize this fact: Colossians 3:11; Galatians 3:28; 1 Corinthians 12:13; John 10:16; 17:11; Ephesians 2:14-15.

2. Look up the following scriptures which refer to judgement, and describe the results of that great day: Matthew 16:27; Acts 10:42; Romans 2:16; 14:10-12; 2 Corinthians 5:10; Ephesians 6:8.

3. Even slaves who are believers have an inheritance in Christ. Look up the following scriptures and make notes about this promised reward: Acts 20:32; Romans 8:17; 1 Peter 1:3-5.

The responsibilities of masters

As we have just seen, it is not only slaves who will be punished for the wrong they have done, because God is no respecter of persons

(Colossians 3:25); masters will also be judged and will be rewarded or punished for their actions in this life.

The slave owner who becomes a Christian must ensure that his new standing affects the whole of his life. Even his slaves, whom perhaps he formerly treated with contempt, should be able to notice a marked difference in his behaviour towards everyone with whom he has to deal. He is to treat his slaves in ways that are right and fair. He knows that this will bring him into conflict with his fellow slave owners; they may well regard him as unwise to reward his slaves. They will certainly accuse him of encouraging the slaves to demand better conditions from their masters. Nevertheless, because the Christian slave owner has been saved and 'renewed in his mind', he will no longer act in accordance with 'the pattern of this world' (Romans 12:2).

One of the members of the church at Colosse, Philemon, owned at least one slave. His slave was Onesimus who had run away, but who came into contact with Paul during the apostle's imprisonment. Onesimus became a Christian, and he knew that he should return to his master. It was Paul's desire that Philemon should receive his slave back, 'no longer as a slave, but better than a slave, as a dear brother' (Philemon 16).

Christian employees and employers

The principles that Paul outlines in these verses are still relevant. Christian people are required to work conscientiously whether it will enhance their promotion prospects or not. They will not take unnecessarily long breaks, even if the supervisor is out of the room. Neither will they deliberately seek to show their fellow-employees in a poor light because they have worked more hours solely for the purpose of pleasing their employer.

All the work they do will be done sincerely, out of reverence for the Lord. Four times in chapter 3:22-24 the Lord's name is mentioned. It is not the employee's promotion prospects — nor even the dividend payment received by the employer — that ultimately matters. The thing that is paramount is that the Lord receives the glory.

Just as the Christian slaver owner was to provide for his slaves that which was right and fair, so Christian employers must treat their workers with justice. They must not exploit them in any way.

The Christian employer's main aim should be the glory of God; and God is glorified when the gospel is seen at work in the compassionate care of a work force. What is important is that both employer and employee act honestly. An employer sometimes has to keep the state of his business secret, because a rival company might well make a 'take over bid' without his knowledge or consent. Nevertheless, the employer, who is aware that he or she has to reduce the size of his work force, should not hide the true situation from his employees any longer than he need do so. Otherwise, they might be prevented from obtaining alternative employment elsewhere. The Christian knows that his duty is to treat his workers well, because he has a Master in heaven who is watching him.

SUMMARIZE IT

We have seen so far that even slaves and masters have duties to each other, but especially to the Lord. This portion of scripture has great relevance to workers and employers today.

QUESTION TIME

1. *In Christ, everyone is promised freedom. He was sent into the world to proclaim freedom for the prisoners (Luke 4:18). In which ways have Christians been freed today? (Romans 6:18,22; 1 Corinthians 9:18; Hebrews 2:15; 9:15). In what situations are they still bound? (1 Peter 2:16; 2 Peter 2:19; 1 Corinthians 9:21).*

2. *How are we to treat those believers who have fewer educational qualifications or business skills than we do? If they do not conform to our patterns of social behaviour, should we avoid inviting them into our homes for fear of embarrassing them? (Acts 10:34-35; Deuteronomy 10:17; 2 Chronicles 19:7; Job 34:18-19;*

Mark 12:14; Romans 2:11; Galatians 2:6; Ephesians 6:9; James 2:1-7; 1 Peter 1:17).

CHAPTER NINETEEN

THE MYSTERY OF CHRIST PROCLAIMED

(BIBLE **READING**)

Colossians 4:2-6

Having laid a good foundation of truth and having urged the Colossians not to be deceived by those who claimed to have a greater understanding of truth than the apostles, Paul now proceeds to write his closing thoughts.

Praying to God fervently and for outsiders

How would the Colossian Christians cope when faced with the superior intellect of these false teachers who had come among them? They would do so by being grounded in the truth, the truth that Epaphras had preached to them (1:7), and by prayer. This was not a question of merely 'saying' or reciting prayers which had previously been learned 'off by heart'. The Colossians were to 'devote' themselves to prayer. It was to take up much of their spare time, and also to be engaged in during break-times in their working day. Unlike the disciples who went to sleep in the garden of Gethsemane, they were to be watchful (Matthew 26:36-46).

They were also to be thankful when they prayed. This was because they knew that God always hears and answers prayer. They were not like those who had no hope (1:27). They were to pray with thanksgiving, knowing that God always watched over them and cared for them. They knew, too, that prayer for others was effective.

In urging them to pray, Paul greatly desired that they pray for him too. He did not ask them to pray that the prison doors might swing open so that he could go free. He prayed that God would open a door for his message. His big desire, even in the discomfort and frustration of being in prison, was that the mystery of Christ (which had been kept secret for such a long time) should be proclaimed. There is no suggestion that Paul wanted to proclaim the gospel merely out of duty. His strong desire was that he might proclaim it clearly, as he knew he should. We, too, should proclaim that message with great boldness and clarity.

PRACTICAL TASKS

1. Study the parable of the persistent widow in Luke 18:1-8 and note down what you learn about the need to be persistent in prayer. See also Acts 1:14; 2:42 and 1 Thessalonians 5:17.

2. Read Joshua chapter 4 and note how the stones of remembrance reminded Joshua of God's goodness to him and his

people. Make a list of those things that bring to mind tokens of God's love to you in the past as well as in the present, and thank him for those blessings that he has promised for the future.

3. Look up some of the passages in which Paul records how doors had opened for the mystery of the gospel which had been hidden for so long to be revealed. See Acts 14:26-28; Romans 16:25; 1 Corinthians 16:8-9; 2 Corinthians 2:12; Revelation 3:8.

Speaking to people about God

Not every Christian has been called to preach from a pulpit; but all Christians have the obligation placed upon them to witness to the gospel of God's grace. Sadly, some are preaching sermons in churches and chapels today who do not have the ability or the authority of God to do so. Some preachers and many Christian believers bring the gospel into disrepute because of the clumsy way in which they witness for the Lord. Obviously, it was the same in Paul's day because he called upon the Colossians to 'be wise in the way [they acted] towards outsiders'.

Not only can believers be unwise in the words they speak to unsaved people, they can also be unwise in the way they act. The person who speaks the words of the gospel message, yet lives a life which is not in keeping with that message,

WHAT THE TEXT TEACHES

is doing harm to the cause of Christ. The way we think and act must be in line with what we say. In their eagerness to 'make the most of every opportunity', some are speaking without careful thought about the consequence of their words. The emphasis that Paul gives here is not so much on Christians rushing in with something to say, it is on the need for believers to be able to listen carefully to what the unsaved person says, and then to give him or her a biblical answer that will cause that person to think of Christ and his claims.

Whatever we say, whether it is in a situation where there is an opening to witness to the truth of the gospel, or in response to a question asked by an outsider, we must always let our conversation (our actions as well as our words) be full of grace. We must speak in such a way that will cause our hearer to find our words interesting, thought-provoking and helpful.

God gives ample instruction on how to live wisely (Ephesians 5:2,15-21; 4:32; Philippians 2:14-16; 1 Thessalonians 4:1-7), and the Lord Jesus Christ said that his followers are 'the salt of the earth' (Matthew 5:13). Before refrigeration was invented, salt was used as a preservative. It was also used to cleanse wounds, and still today it is invaluable in flavouring our food. We, as God's people, are to live our lives (i.e., our conversation) 'full of grace' and 'seasoned with salt'. We should be a blessing to those whom we meet. We should act as a cleansing agent in this evil world, and we should give flavour to the things which happen around us and the language which is used in our presence.

SUMMARIZE IT

We have seen so far that we need to pray for those who preach the Word and also engage in wise conversation with the unsaved around us, so that we can answer their questions and point them to the gospel of saving grace.

QUESTION TIME

DISCUSS IT

1. *How can we pray with thanksgiving when we are in painful and distressing circumstances? Read Paul's prayers in these 'prison epistles' (Ephesians 1:15-23; 3:14-21; Philippians 1:3-11; Colossians 1:3-6).*

2. *How do you answer those who become offended when you tell them that they are sinners, in danger of the judgement of God at the last day? (Proverbs 22:17-21; Isaiah 58:9; Luke 21:14-15; 1 Peter 3:15).*

CHAPTER TWENTY

THE
CHRISTIAN'S
FRIENDS

BIBLE READING

Colossians 4:7-18

WHAT THE TEXT TEACHES

How do people manage if they have no friends? When a tragedy occurs, it is the presence and the words and gifts of friends that count a great deal. The Christian has many friends in the church. These are even closer friends than one's natural family members who are outside of Christ, because Christians are all one in Christ' (Galatians 3:28).

Paul ends this letter with a list of greetings to his many Christian friends. This list is longer than in any of Paul's other letters, with the exception of the epistle to the Romans. As we read through these closing verses, we notice that the apostle speaks with such tenderness about each of the people he mentions — with the exception of Demas (4:14). Although he was cut off in prison, he was not separated from the love of the Lord, or his Christian friends. They were very dear to him; together, they had gone through so much. He especially mentions the faithfulness of several of these people. Loyalty may be a quality that is missing in the rush of everyday life in

the twenty-first century, yet Tychicus (4:7), Onesimus
(4:9) and Epaphras (4:12) are especially singled out by
Paul because he had found them dependable and faithful to the work of the gospel.

Some of Paul's friends were with him in prison:
Aristarchus and Mark were there (4:10), and it seems
that Luke and Demas were too (4:14). They were keen
to stay with Paul but, as much as he valued the company of Tychicus and Onesimus, he sent them to the
believers at Colosse and the surrounding area.

(PRACTICAL TASKS)

1. Tychicus is mentioned five times in the New Testament. Look
   up these references and write down what we are told about
   Tychicus: Acts 20:4; Ephesians 6:21; 2 Timothy 4:12 and
   Titus 3:12.

2. Onesimus was also a friend of Paul. Look through the letter
   to Philemon and also Colossians 4:9 and make notes about
   this man.

Paul had three Jews with him: Aristarchus, Mark and
Jesus, called Justus (4:11). It would seem that all the
other Jews where Paul was, had refused to accept that
he had been sent by God. However, these three stood
by him and were a great comfort to him in his 'chains'
and in his distress.

Many times Paul must have felt frustrated, especially
when he heard that things were going wrong in the
churches. He would have loved to have visited these

people and explained the issues face to face, and presented them with the truths of the gospel message. He had been told about false teachers who had wormed their way into the churches and promised 'fulness' without the simplicity of the gospel. Nevertheless, the apostle had as his weapon the pen, and he proved that it was mightier than the sword. For him, in his day, it was the equivalent of the telephone and e-mail in our day. Paul's writings were used to bring the power and the truth of the Word of God to people who were in danger of going astray, and this was because his letters were inspired by God's Spirit.

This letter was not just sent to the church at Colosse; its contents were also to be shared with the neighbouring congregations at Laodicea (it was perhaps in the house of Nympha that this church held its meetings) and also Hierapolis (4:13,15-16). Archippus was already in the area and soon Tychicus and Onesimus would be joining him. They were to encourage him to complete the work to which the Lord had called him.

With these friendly and loving greetings, Paul ends this letter. No doubt he joined in the prayer of Epaphras that these believers at Colosse would 'stand firm in all the will of God,' that they would be 'mature and fully assured' (4:12).

PRACTICAL TASKS

1. Epaphras exerted much effort in the work of the gospel. Make a list of his qualities and actions, concentrating on words such as 'faithful minister' (he spoke to Paul about the Colossians, 1:8), 'wrestling in prayer' (he prayed for the Colossians, 4:12), 'working hard' (he worked for the Colossians, 4:13). Note also that he was a 'prisoner' (Philemon 23) and a citizen of Colosse (Colossians 4:12).

2. Demas also was with Paul and sent his greetings. Find out what happened to Demas later when Paul wrote what was probably his final letter (2 Timothy 4:10).

QUESTION TIME

1. Which two tasks did Paul especially entrust to Tychicus and Onesimus (4:7-9)? And how may we, today, encourage others in the work of the gospel? (Ephesians 6:21-22; Colossians 2:2; Titus 1:9; Hebrews 3:13, 10:25.)

2. Paul included Mark and Demas in these closing greetings. Mark fell away (Acts 15:37-38), but was brought back (2 Timothy 4:11). It seems that Demas departed completely (2 Timothy 4:10). Why do some people turn back from the path that God has called them to?

3. How can we 'stand firm' in the faith of the gospel? *(1 Corinthians 15:58; 16:13; 2 Corinthians 1:21; 2:9; Galatians 5:1; Ephesians 6:13: Philippians 1:27; 2 Timothy 2:15; 1 Peter 5:12).*

CHAPTER TWENTY-ONE

INTRODUCTION
TO
PHILEMON

BIBLE READING

Philemon 1-25

WHAT THE TEXT TEACHES

Of the twenty-one letters in the New Testament, only five or six are written to individuals, some of the other letters are written to churches. Those written to individuals are the two letters to Timothy, the letter to Titus, this little one to Philemon and the third letter of John (written to Gaius, 3 John 1). 2 John is addressed to 'the chosen lady' (2 John 1) who may or may not have been a specific person.[1] The letters to Timothy and Titus are often called the Pastoral Epistles because they are written to the leaders of churches (at Ephesus and Crete), giving them much guidance and instruction on how they should lead their churches in a biblical and God-honouring way.

However, this letter to Philemon is of an entirely different nature. From verses 4–21 the words 'you' and 'yours' are in the singular. This is because they are addressed personally to the wealthy slave owner Philemon. This letter is far more personal than anything in the Pastoral Epistles. So, does this mean that we are being rude to read it if it is not addressed to us?

Certainly it would seem, from the way in which these middle verses are written, that we ought to avert our eyes. However, when we examine the words 'you' and 'yours' in verse 3 and in verses 22 and 25, we discover that they are in the plural. Although this is a personal letter, it is also written to 'Apphia our sister, to Archippus our fellow-soldier and to the church' that meets in Philemon's home (v. 2).

Philemon is a man who is rich enough to own slaves, and also to have a house large enough in which believers can gather for worship and fellowship. As has been stated, it is clear that it is the church in the home of Philemon (v. 2) which is being referred to in verse 3 and also in verses 22 and 25. So, although this is a personal letter to Philemon, it is one that is intended to be read to Philemon's fellow-believers. This also means that in the twenty-first century we are entitled to 'glance over Philemon's shoulder' and see what the apostle has written. This is because we, too, belong to the church of Jesus Christ (if we have truly been born again), and the principles of love and reconciliation are ones that we should all learn and obey.

Philemon is saved

We do not know how Philemon became a Christian, but it is not inconceivable that, in the course of his work, he sometimes had to travel to Ephesus: the large and busy seaport that served as the business centre for the whole region. We have already seen that Paul taught

WHAT THE TEXT TEACHES

for a period of about two years in the hall of
Tyrannus in that city (Acts 19:9). During that
time, many people were brought out of darkness
into the light of the gospel (Colossians 1:13);
Philemon may well have been included among
them.

As Paul calls Philemon 'our dear friend and
fellow-worker' (v. 1), it seems that they knew each
other well. Being a businessman, he would have
been well educated, and perhaps that drew him
to the learned apostle. We certainly know that
Philemon became a keen Christian worker (v. 1).

When he returned home, he was most enthusi-
astic about his new-found faith, and he told many
people about his Lord and Master. As a result,
others came to trust in the Lord as their Saviour
too. This may explain why a church started to
meet in the home of Philemon; it was not likely
that there would have been religious buildings
open to them, and any that there were would have
been devoted to heathen deities.

Onesimus is saved

Among the slaves that Philemon owned one was
called Onesimus. His name means 'useful' and,
no doubt, he worked hard for his master. We can
imagine that when Philemon was saved, he came
home with a much kinder attitude to everyone

than he had had before. He would probably have treated his slaves better than other slave owners.

We do not know whether Onesimus took advantage of Philemon's more generous nature or not, but he certainly ran away — probably taking money with him (see v. 18). We do not know how he arrived at the place where Paul was imprisoned, which was probably the imperial city of Rome. However, because he had committed two grievous crimes — running away and stealing — he was in danger of being caught and, maybe, even being put to death. Therefore, he had to take great care that no one found out his true identity or background.

But 'God moves in a mysterious way, his wonders to perform' and somehow Onesimus came face to face with the apostle Paul. Perhaps he obtained work helping to clean prisons. We do not know the details; but we are certain of this: he not only met Paul, but he met Paul's Saviour as well; and, as a result, Onesimus came to faith in Christ.

PRACTICAL TASKS

1. Look up Acts 19:23-27 and read the testimony of Demetrius who was complaining about loss of trade because, as he said, 'Paul has convinced and led astray large numbers of people here in Ephesus, and in practically the whole province of Asia' (19:26). Colosse was in the Roman province of Asia.

2. Look back to what was said about the duties of slaves (see chapter 18).

3. The meaning of Onesimus' name is referred to in verses 11 and 20. Note down some of the things that Paul has to say about Onesimus being useful and of benefit to him.

4. Find a copy of William Cooper's hymn, the first stanza of which reads like this:

God moves in a mysterious way
His wonders to perform;
He plants his footsteps in the sea,
And rides upon the storm.

Onesimus desires to put matters right with Philemon

Whenever a person comes to faith in Christ, that person's whole life and outlook changes completely. One of the things that happens is that that person is conscious of the sin he or she has committed against the Lord and also the wrongs that have been done to other people. The conscience has been pricked and the person wants to do everything he or she can to make amends for previously bad behaviour.

Surely Onesimus would have felt like this. Certainly, Paul would have taught him that if the Lord had forgiven him, then he must seek to put right any wrong he had done to others. This meant that he must ask forgiveness from Philemon. This would not have been easy for him because he was guilty of grievous crimes: desertion and stealing.

Although Paul sent him back to Philemon (v. 12), Onesimus must have been a willing partner in this venture. The whole purpose of this letter is to urge Philemon to have mercy on Onesimus and receive him back 'no longer as a slave, but better than a slave, as a dear brother' (vv. 15-16). These very bold words of Paul are sent with warmth and loving zeal, both for Philemon and for his slave. He is so sure of Philemon's acceptance of Onesimus that he can write confidently of Philemon's obedience to his apostolic request.

SUMMARIZE IT

We have seen so far that this letter was written by Paul to Philemon whose slave Onesimus had fled and had come into contact with the apostle. There, he had become a Christian and, under Paul's influence, he had desired to return to seek his master's forgiveness.

QUESTION TIME

1. What principles do we find in the Bible to help us when we need to write a letter in which it is necessary to

point out the faults of a fellow Christian? (Galatians 6:1-5; Matthew 18:15-17; Leviticus 19:17-18; Luke 17:3; 2 Corinthians 2:5-8).

2. *How does Jesus' teaching in Luke 15:11-21 compare with the experience of Onesimus? (See also Psalm 51:4; Isaiah 17:7-8; Ezekiel 33:11; Acts 3:19; Revelation 2:5).*

3. *What kinds of things prevent us from seeking forgiveness from those we have wronged? (Proverbs 8:13; Matthew 15:19; Malachi 3:7-13).*

THE GUIDE

CHAPTER TWENTY-TWO

THE
IMPORTANCE
OF FAITH
AND LOVE

LOOK IT UP

BIBLE READING

Philemon 1-7

WHAT THE TEXT TEACHES

The Greeting (1-3)

Paul follows the custom of his day and starts his letter with his own name. At the beginning of most of his letters, including the one to Colosse, he described himself as 'an apostle of Christ Jesus by the will of God'. However, here he merely describes himself as 'a prisoner of Christ Jesus'. He does not call himself a 'prisoner of Rome', but 'a prisoner of Christ Jesus'. Physically, he was at the mercy of the Roman authorities who had him in chains (Philemon 10,13), but spiritually he was bound to the Lord Jesus Christ. Four times in this short letter Paul refers to his imprisonment (vv. 1,9,13,23). We know that the main reason why Paul wrote this letter was to urge Philemon to forgive his runaway slave and receive him as a brother in Christ. Already, in the very first verse, the apostle has started to prepare Philemon to see that his slave, Onesimus, was not really owned by Philemon; his real Master was the Lord.

While this is Paul's letter, as in the case of the Colossian letter, he also sends it from Timothy, whom he describes as 'our brother' (i.e., Timothy is a brother in Christ both to Paul and to Philemon, and also to all of those who are in the family of God).

We have noticed in the previous chapter of this book that Paul refers to Philemon as 'our dear friend and fellow-worker'. He is using the same brotherly terms which he has used with respect to Timothy. Paul goes on to greet Apphia 'our sister' and Archippus 'our fellow-soldier'. Some feel that Apphia is Philemon's wife and Archippus his son. While there is no strong evidence to support this, Paul certainly continues the sentence by saying, '…and to the church that meets in your home.' On the other hand, in Colossians 4:17, Archippus is mentioned immediately after the reference to the neighbouring church of Laodicea. Paul urges Archippus to 'see to it that [he] completes the work [he has] received in the Lord'. From this statement, some have concluded that Archippus lived at Laodicea and exercised his ministry as a fellow-soldier in that city. Whatever the case, Laodicea and Colosse were within walking distance of each other (see map on page 2).

As usual, Paul wishes the church in Philemon's house 'grace … and peace'. Both of these blessings are sent 'from God our Father and the Lord Jesus Christ'. It is not from Paul or any other apostle that people receive

God's blessings; it is from God alone that grace and peace come.

PRACTICAL TASKS

WORK AT IT

1. Paul addressed the believing brothers and sisters. This is not just a friendly way of greeting one another, it is an indication that every true Christian belongs to the family of God. Look up the following scripture references to note this point: Hebrews 2:11; Galatians 6:10; Ephesians 3:15; 1 Peter 4:17.

2. Read carefully through Romans 5:1-11 and notice how the grace of God produces peace in the life of the believer.

3. Write out the following verses, making a note of what Paul gives thanks for in each one: Romans 1:8; 1 Corinthians 1:4; Ephesians 1:16; 1 Thessalonians 2:13; 2 Thessalonians 1:3; 2 Timothy 1:3.

The Thanksgiving

Paul exercises much tact as he moves towards the request that he wishes to make of Philemon. However, there is nothing degrading or insincere in these verses. What Paul is telling Philemon is the truth. He always thanks God for Philemon and remembers him in his prayers; and he does not grow weary in this exercise because he hears news of Philemon from time to time. What he hears encourages him to thank God more fervently.

The two things that he learns about Philemon concern his faith and his love. Faith never stands alone; we must always have faith in something or someone. Paul makes it clear that Philemon's faith is not in himself or his abilities — not even in Paul. His faith is in the Lord Jesus Christ. Because of this faith in the Lord, he is enabled to show love to all the saints. He does not merely love those believers who give him pleasure, he loves them all, whatever their background or present condition.

Paul goes on to encourage Philemon to continue to show these virtues. He prays that Philemon may be active in sharing his faith, so that he will have 'a full understanding of every good thing we have in Christ'. Here 'fulness' is mentioned again (i.e., the Colossian heresy). Paul tells Philemon that he is praying that he will know fulness — not because some false teachers have promised it, but because he is trusting in the Lord Jesus Christ alone to grant this. James tells us that 'every good and perfect gift is from above' (James 1:17).

Although Paul is suffering the deprivation and discomfort of prison, he is full of joy because 'brother' Philemon, the wealthy employer, has 'refreshed the hearts of the saints'. Throughout these verses (4-7), Paul makes it clear that this is a personal message from himself to Philemon. He repeats 'my', 'me' and 'I', and he refers to Philemon in terms of 'you' and 'your'.

DISCUSS IT

1. How can you love a fellow Christian with whom you have had a severe disagreement? (Matthew 5:23-24; Philippians 2:1-4; Romans 12:9-13; Philippians 4:2).

2. What are the benefits of Christian love? (1 Peter 4:8; Philippians 1:9-11: 1 Thessalonians 3:12-13).

3. How can believers guard against being unproductive in their Christian lives? (2 Peter 1:5-9; John 15:2; Colossians 1:10; Titus 3:14).

CHAPTER
TWENTY-THREE

THE BLESSINGS
OF SLAVERY

BIBLE READING

Philemon 8-14

The main purpose of the letter
(vv. 8-11)

It is not until verse 8 that Paul finally starts to deal with the central issue of his letter. He commences with the word 'therefore'. In other words, he has been saying many pleasant and true things about Philemon, but he now wants Philemon to demonstrate further the love that he has (because of his faith in Christ). He says, 'Although in Christ I could be bold and order you to do what you ought to do, yet I appeal to you on the basis of love' (v. 8).

So far, in this letter, he has made no mention of his apostolic authority. Now he alludes to it, but he is still not going to demand obedience — even though he has the right to do so. His appeal is on the grounds of Christian love and Christian family loyalty. However, before he mentions the name of Philemon's runaway slave, Paul draws attention to two matters concerning himself. He tells him that he is old (scholars think he was around 60 years of age) and also that he is in prison, and all this 'for Christ's sake'. It was because of his loyalty to Christ and his desire to suffer for him that he had been incarcerated.

Finally, 145 words into this letter of 335 words[1], Paul makes mention of the runaway slave Onesimus. Was Philemon angry when he heard the name of the one who had abused his kindness? We do not know. All we have here is Paul's appeal to Philemon to forgive and receive back into his household the one who had wronged him. Paul is appealing to Philemon to forgive his slave; but he does so most graciously. He refers to Onesimus as 'my son ... who became my son while I was in chains' (v. 10). Once again Paul uses family terms. This was to remind Philemon that when anyone is saved that person enters into an entirely new relationship with Christ and with other believers. They all become brothers and sisters in Christ. Paul had been the instrument that God had used to lead Onesimus to faith in Christ, and therefore he became his son. Notice, too, that twice Paul uses the heart-rending words, 'I appeal to you' (vv. 9-10).

The apostle then proceeds to make a play on Onesimus' name. We have already seen that his name means 'useful'. In the past, Philemon had, apparently, found his slave to be useless, but we have no details about this. Perhaps it was the fact that he had run away and had possibly stolen something belonging to his master that Paul had in mind when he said that Onesimus had been useless to Philemon. However, the apostle then goes on to say that although he had been useless to Philemon in the past, 'now he has become useful both to you and to me'. Since his conversion, Onesimus had been of great assistance to Paul; and the apostle knew that, as a new man in Christ, Onesimus would prove to be useful to his master in the future.

Conversion to Christ always brings about a complete change in a person. In his life as a non-Christian, the unsaved person is under the dominion of darkness (Colossians 1:13); his natural inclination is devoted to following 'the ways of this world' which, in turn, lead him or her to 'gratifying the cravings of [the] sinful nature and following its desires and thoughts' (Ephesians 2:2-3). This means that, with regard to service for the Lord and his church, such people are useless because their activity is devoted to their own selfish ends, rather than to the glory of God.

Before he was saved, Paul himself thought that he was being a useful servant of God. He considered that the whole of his upbringing and behaviour were to his profit; but a great transformation took place in him when he met Christ on the road to Damascus. Then he came to view all of those previous achievements as 'rubbish' (Philippians 3:5-9). Since being called by God, he had become useful to a wide range of people. From reading his letters and also the book of Acts, we find many examples of how God used him, and continues to do so all these many centuries later.

Even as Christians, particularly when we are feeling downcast, we may consider ourselves to be useless to God and his people. But if we accept the responsibility laid upon us by the call of the gospel, then we will prove to be helpful in many ways that we may not have previously considered feasible. At one time, Paul found Mark to be unworthy of continuing with him in his missionary enterprises (Acts 15:37,39), but the time came, near the end of his life, when he wrote that Mark was 'helpful to me in my ministry (2 Timothy 4:11).

Others, too, may look at us as believers and think that we have nothing constructive to offer to the work of the Lord. That was how the members of the London Missionary Society considered the young Gladys Aylward when she told them of her 'call' to work in China. They felt that she would not be able to cope; she was useless because she was not well educated. However, as history has shown, in God's hands, she became a great and powerful servant of the Lord, proving her usefulness in the lives of many Chinese children and leading hundreds of them to safety from the Japanese invasion of the late 1930s.

PRACTICAL TASKS

1. Make a note of some of the benefits that came from Paul's imprisonment (see Acts 20:23; 21:33 – 22:1; 22:29; Ephesians 6:20; 2 Timothy 2:9).

2. Find out what you can about Tychicus. Refer to Acts 20:4; Ephesians 6:21; Colossians 4:7; 2 Timothy 4:12 and Titus 3:12.

3. Note the warm language of relationship that Paul uses as he pleads to Philemon to forgive Onesimus: 'my son', (v. 10), 'my very heart' (v. 12) and 'a dear brother' (v. 16). Compare this with Exodus 32:32 where Moses pleads with God to forgive the many sins of the Israelites.

The return of Onesimus (vv. 12-14)

With the letter, Paul sent this runaway slave back to Philemon. During his time with Paul, Onesimus had not only come to faith in Christ, he had also realized that he had a responsibility, as much as possible, to try to put right the wrongs of the past. Therefore, he knew that he must return to his master and ask for his forgiveness. His desire was to seek to make amends for his wrongdoing and be accepted back into Philemon's household and resume his duties.

Onesimus did not return to Colosse thinking that, as he was now converted, he was 'free in Christ'. Therefore, Philemon had an obligation to forgive him and release him from his former work. On the contrary, he went back in humility with two things to encourage him: Paul's blessing and commendation, and the companionship of Tychicus (Colossians 4:7-9). Tychicus had a wealth of Christian experience and was highly commended by Paul. He was a fine servant of the Lord, a good brother in Christ. This means that he must also have been a blessed companion and teacher to Onesimus.

Paul continues to speak highly of Onesimus. We have already noted that he says that Onesimus is not only '[his] son' who is 'useful to [him]', but he is also '[his] very heart'. The apostle further commends him by saying that he would like to keep him with him so that 'he can take your place in helping me while I am in chains for the gospel'.

Despite Paul's apostolic authority, and the high esteem in which he was held by all, he did not presume to act without Philemon's permission with respect to someone who belonged to Philemon. Out of politeness, he did not demand that he be allowed to keep Onesimus with him; he desired Philemon's consent to keep Onesimus and he also wishes Philemon to act in a spontaneous way, without any feeling of compulsion, or even suggestion, from Paul.

Those who have any authority in the church, be it as a Sunday school teacher, a deacon or an elder should not be in a hurry to tell their 'charges' what they should do. Certainly, they should instruct them in the teaching of God's Word, but they should then leave them to act in accordance with the Bible's teaching and their own consciences. The apostle Peter recognizes the need to act graciously in these kinds of circumstances. He pleads, not as an apostle, but as a fellow-elder, as he urges elders of churches not to lord it over those entrusted to their care (1 Peter 5:1-4).

SUMMARIZE IT

We have seen so far how Paul pleads with Philemon to forgive his runaway slave and receive him back. Paul highly values the service of Onesimus and he trusts that Philemon will discover that, since his slave has come to Christ, he has become a highly useful servant.

QUESTION TIME

DISCUSS IT

1. What can strengthen our usefulness for the Lord and his work? (Joshua 1:7; 1 Corinthains 3:6-11; 15:58; Philippians 2:1-5).

2. How can we put into practice the Bible's teaching on servanthood? (Galatians 5:13; 1 Corinthians. 9:19; 2 Corinthians 4:5).

3. In which ways should love control our thoughts and actions? (Ephesians 4:2,15; Romans 13:9; 1 Corinthians 13:6; Colossians 3:14; 1 John 3:11).

CHAPTER
TWENTY-FOUR

THE BLESSING
OF
RESTORATION

THE G U I D E

BIBLE READING

Philemon 15-25

WHAT THE TEXT TEACHES

Further reasons to forgive (vv. 15-21)

Although it might well be difficult for Philemon to forgive his slave and receive him back into his household, his respect for Paul would have encouraged him to listen to the pleas of the apostle.

Paul would have been very conscious that if Philemon forgave his runaway slave and received him back into his household, then it would almost certainly have caused Philemon's fellow slave owners to raise their eyebrows in disbelief. Furthermore, they would argue that this action could appear to make it possible for other slaves to claim that they had become Christians and expect to received similar treatment.

This is probably one of the reasons why Paul explains that Onesimus is not the same person as he was when he ran away. He now has a new Master: the same Lord that Philemon serves. He has demonstrated to Paul's satisfaction that he is a new man in Christ. Paul is satisfied that Onesimus is truly sorry for the wrong that he has committed against Philemon, and he knows that he sincerely wants to make amends for all the harm he has done. Philemon could use these kinds of statements to explain to his friends why he was willing to receive Onesimus back into his household.

Churches, too, should require that 'backsliders' who wish to come back into the fellowship demonstrate that they are truly repentant. Words are not enough. Many unbelievers, and Christians too, who have drifted away from the ways of God, know which words they should say to wheedle their way into the church membership, but the Lord requires fruit to be shown. Jesus said, 'By their fruit you will recognize them' (Matthew 7:16), and Paul tells Agrippa that he preached that people should 'repent and turn to God *and prove their repentance by their deeds*' (Act 26:20, italics mine).

Paul is not saying, 'Have him back until he runs away again, or he is too old to do useful work.' He is saying that Philemon should have him back for good, 'no longer as a slave, but better than a slave, as a dear brother' (v. 16). Then the apostle says that, as dear as Onesimus is to him, he will be even dearer to Philemon, not now as a slave, but as 'a man, and as a brother in the Lord' (v. 16).

There is no doubt that Philemon would have great pleasure in welcoming Paul into his household; the apostle knew that he would gladly prepare a guest room for him (v. 22). Therefore, the apostle's reasoning is this: if Philemon considered me, Paul, as a partner in the work of the gospel, then he should also welcome Onesimus back into his household, in the same way that he would welcome me. Should there still be lingering doubts in Philemon's mind, Paul would even be willing to repay any wrong that Onesimus had done to his master. And the reason he is prepared to do this is because Onesimus is very dear to him.

Then, to reinforce the truth of what he is saying, Paul takes the pen out of the hands of the person who is actually writing the letter, and, in his own handwriting, he signs an IOU. In effect, he writes something that could be interpreted like this: 'I will pay back anything that Onesimus owes you. But don't forget that you are indebted to me, in the sense that I led you to Christ and to fulness of life. You have often wanted to repay me for preaching the gospel to you. All right then, repay me by receiving Onesimus back and forgiving him. This will refresh my heart in Christ. But I know what a big heart you have. For this reason, I am confident that you will obey my wishes. In fact, knowing your generous nature, I am sure that you will do far more than I even dare to ask you.'

Personal, practical matters (vv. 22-25)

So Paul draws this unique and intimate letter to a close. 'And one thing more,' he adds, 'prepare a guest room for me, because I hope to be restored to you in answer to your prayer.' Paul was reminding Philemon that God answers prayer.

Paul is also thanking him for his diligence in praying for him while he has been imprisoned.

As usual, the apostle mentions those who send their greetings. In his humility, Paul writes as though the recipient of his letter will be more interested in the others who are with him than in himself. He mentions five in particular.

We have already looked at some of the activities of Epaphras (Colossians 1:7; 4:12; Philemon 23). It was in the house of Mark's mother that the people gathered to pray for Peter's release from prison (Acts 12:12,25). It is very interesting to note that it was this same John Mark who had deserted Paul when they were on a missionary journey together in Pamphilyia. Instead, it was Barnabas who took Mark 'under his wing' (Acts 15:37,39). Perhaps Philemon knew the story and Paul was hinting about the fact that he eventually took Mark back and found him to be a valuable companion (2 Timothy 4:11; Colossians 4:10). Peter also valued Mark's company (1 Peter 5:13).

We know very little about Aristarchus, except that he was a valued companion of Paul. In Colossians 4:10, he is described as Paul's 'fellow-prisoner' (Acts 19:29; 20:4; 27:2; Colossians 4:10; Philemon 24). Although Demas was also one of Paul's companions (Colossians 4:14; Philemon 24), he eventually went in the opposite direction to Mark. Near the end of Paul's life, with sadness, he told Timothy that 'Demas has deserted me' because 'he loved his world' (2 Timothy 4:10). Finally, he mentions Luke. In Colossians 4:14, Paul described Luke as 'our dear friend... the doctor'. In 2 Timothy

4:11 he is Paul's sole companion in what is likely to be his final days in prison. As the author of Luke's Gospel and the Acts of the Apostles, we also glean more information about this meticulous man (e.g., he 'carefully investigated everything from the beginning ... and he wrote an orderly account' of the gospel of Jesus Christ (Luke 1:3).

The letter ends with a brief but blessed benediction: 'The grace of the Lord Jesus Christ be with your spirit.'

PRACTICAL TASKS

1. The Bible gives us a number of illustrations of how good has come out of difficult circumstances. Read the story of Joseph in Genesis chapters 37 and 39-50, and notice Joseph's words to his brothers in Genesis 50:20.

SUMMARIZE IT

Paul pleads with Philemon to take back his slave Onesimus. He guarantees that Philemon will be blessed if he forgives this brother; and it will also give Paul much pleasure to see Onesimus serving Philemon, not as a slave but as a hard-working man and a dear Christian brother.

WORK AT IT

QUESTION TIME

1. *Paul, as an apostle, had the right (the authority) to demand Philemon's obedience. Should we always demand to be treated in accordance with our rights? (Hebrews 5:8; Philippians 2:6-8; 1 Peter 5:5; Ephesians 5:21).*

2. *One of the best-loved Christian books is The Pilgrim's Progress. John Bunyan wrote this while he was in prison for preaching without a licence; he was in prison from 1660-1672. How is it possible to produce more 'fruit' for the glory of God when you are busy in his service or when you are quietly waiting on him? (Mark 6:31; Luke 10:38-42; Exodus 14:14; Isaiah 41:1 and Psalm 37:7).*

3. *What have you learned about the blessings of forgiveness through studying this book? (Matthew 18:21-22; 6:12).*

NOTES

END   NOTES

REFERENCES

Chapter 1. Writing the letter to the church at Colosse
1. R. Kent Hughes, *Colossians and Philemon*, Crossway Books, Illinois, USA, 1989, p.14

Chapter 2. Opening Greetings
1. Robert W. Wall, *Colossians and Philemon*, I.V.P., 1993, p.38

Chapter 3. The effects of the gospel message
1. R. C. Lucas, *The Message of Colossians and Philemon*, I.V.P. 1980 p.34

Chapter 4. Spiritual prayer
1. The hymn by James Montgomery which starts 'Prayer is the soul's sincere desire.'

Chapter 5. The supremacy of Christ
1. R. C. Lucas, p.49
2. *Ibid*, p.50

Chapter 6. The effects of Christ's shed blood
1. In *Economic and Philosophical Manuscripts of 1844*, Marx developed the notion of the alienation of man under captialism.

Chapter 9. Fulness in Christ
1. quoted in R. Kent Hughes, p.61.
2. Tillandsia plants are a form of Bromeliads, which are mainly rainforest epiphytes. They have 'leaves covered in tiny scales that enable them to retain and absorb moisture and nutrients from the atmosphere' (*A-Z Encyclopaedia of Garden Plants*, Royal Horticultural Society, 1996, p. 47)

Chapter 10. True and false religion
1. R. Kent Hughes, p.72

Chapter 12. From death to life
1. R. C. Lucas, pp.108-109

Chapter 14. The Christian mindset
1. This phrase, and the ideas contained in this work are from R. C. Lucas, p.137
2. H. M. Carson, *Colossians and Philemon*, Tyndale New Testament Commentaries, Tyndale Press, 1960, p. 81

Chapter 15. Put to death old desires
1. R. C. Lucas p.148

Chapter 16. Clothes to put on
1. R. Kent Hughes, p.102
2. W. Barclay, *The letters to the Philippians, Colossians, and Thessalonians*, St Andrew's Press, 1959, p.188
3. R. C. Lucas, p.154

Chapter 17. A Christian's family life
1. William Barclay, p. 192-3
2. John Benton, *Gender Questions, Biblical manhood and woman-hood in the contemporary world*, Evangelical Press,2000, pp.45-63

Chapter 21. Introduction to Philemon
1. 'The chosen lady' may have been a unknown Christian woman or it may have been a description of a church; in Ephesians 5:25 Paul wrote, 'Christ loved the church and gave himself up for *her*.'
2. NIV Study Bible, p. 1874

Chapter 23. The blessings of slavery
1. R. Kent Hughes, p.163